Drops of Nectar

Third Edition

A Collection of Teachings
By
H.H. Swami Chidanand
Saraswatiji Maharaj (Pujya Muniji)

Parmarth Niketan
P.O. Swargashram
Rishikesh (Himalayas)
Uttranchal - 249304, India
Ph.: (0135) 434308, 435300, 434300
Fax: (0135) 434399
E-mail: parmarth@aol.com

621 Illini Drive
Monroeville, PA
15146-1917, USA
Ph: (724) 733 2223
Fax: (724) 733 2224
E-mail: swamiji333@aol.com

This new,
Third Edition of
Drops of Nectar is
sponsored by
**Smt. Sarojben,
Shri Maheshbhai,**
and **Sushri Vaishali
Patel** of Ontario,
Canada in honour
of **Pujya Swamiji's
50th birthday**

H.H. Swami Chidanand Saraswatiji
(Pujya Muniji)

Swami Chidanand Saraswati, 2002,

Drops of Nectar - 3rd Edition

ISBN: 0 9510175 1 9

Cover design by: ***Divine Soul Dawn Baillie, Los Angeles, California.***

Printed at :   *Aravali Printers & Publishers (P) Ltd.* W-30, Okhla Industrial Area, Phase-II, New Delhi-110 020 Phone : 6911417, 6841564, 6931770-3 e-mail : aravali@nde.vsnl.net.in, Website : www.Aravalibooks.com

This book is being offered to you at no charge, as a way of bringing you into closer contact with truth, peace and divinity. **All donations received in connection with this book will go toward Youth Education Services (Y.E.S.),** a non-profit project dedicated to bringing the light of education to the darkness of illiteracy in India. YES is a project of India Heritage Research Foundation, an international humanitarian founded and chaired by Pujya Swami Chidanand Saraswatiji (Muniji). For more information about this and other noble, charitable projects inspired and guided by Pujya Swamiji, please see page 266-276 at the end of this book.

Dear Divine Soul,

May this book fill your life with Drops of inspiration, drops of guidance, drops of wisdom, drops of comfort and drops of divinity.

May you be uplifted and inspired to follow the Divine Path every minute and every moment of every day.

With love and Blessings

In the service of God and humanity

Swami Chidanand Saraswati (Muniji)

CONTENTS

Stories to Touch Your Heart & Teach Your Mind: 159

 PREFACE TO THE THIRD EDITION

It is a great joy and honor to release the third edition of Drops of Nectar on the occasion of H.H. Pujya Swamiji's 50th birthday. When I first met Him, I remember asking Him His age. I did not know at the time that one should not ask this kind of question to a holy man. He, however, responded simply that He was 45. I remember being incredulous at how this holy saint, this clear embodiment of the divine on Earth, this timeless, ageless being could simply be "middle aged." If He had said He was five, I would have believed Him, for His eyes dance and sparkle like a young child's. He moves with the grace and lightness of an angelic, nimble child. Or, if He had said He was five thousand, I also would have believed Him, for His wisdom, His depth of understanding and His omnipotence speak not of a human but of a timeless Being. Yet, forty-five was incomprehensible.

To this day, nearly six years later, it is equally incomprehensible that He is fifty. His eyes dance and sparkle more vibrantly each day. His step becomes lighter, more graceful with each passing year. And yet, simultaneously, His wisdom becomes deeper, more profound, more complete, underscoring everyone's realization that He is simply wearing the clothes of human skin, but is certainly not bound by them.

In fifty years He has accomplished more than most do in many lifetimes. From nearly 10 years of intense sadhana in the forests and Himalayas as a young child, to the years as tireless Sant Narayan Muniji who – even in His early twenties – was given the responsibility of running the largest ashram in Rishikesh, to founding and heading the first Hindu-Jain temple in America, to masterminding the monumental project of the Encyclopedia of Hinduism, to traveling as Gorbachav's guest to the Kremlin for a 7-day Global Forum on peace and the environment, to presiding over Parmarth Niketan Ashram as president for 15 years, turning it into a world-renowned spiritual institution, to representing Hinduism at innumerable international, interfaith conferences, to running over 100 schools, free medical programs, ecological programs, and women's vocational training programs, to giving prayers and blessings in the General Assembly of the United Nations, to meeting with former president Bill Clinton....these are merely glimpses of a life truly lived *"in the service of God and humanity."*

Whenever devotees, who have not seen Him sometimes in decades, come for His darshan, their comments are always the same: "He hasn't changed at all. He looks just like he looked 30 years ago. He's still the same, only better!" Pujya Swamiji seems unaffected by His incredible list of accomplishments and recognitions and remains a humble, pious child of God, owning nothing, draped only in saffron robes, living a life of true renunciation, offering His blessings, His love and Himself to everyone who comes into His presence.

"Mein mast hun, *[I am in divine bliss]*" has been His answer to "How are you?" for over four decades. Whether living in the jungles or living in a mansion..... whether lecturing to a few dozen devotees in the cold, winter morning prayers at Parmarth Niketan or lecturing to thousands of the world's top religious, political, social and business leaders at the World Economic Forum in New York..... whether eating His one begged-for meal a day out of His bare hands as a young wandering sanyasi, or eating a 20 dish meal served to Him on a silver thali in the home of aristocrats..... whether sleeping in a dirt ditch between fields in the Himalayan forests or sleeping in a four post King size bed at the Waldorf Astoria, He is always mast. "*Ast, Vyast, Swast and Mast*...No tension, no depression. Always peaceful, always in ecstasy," is how He describes His life.

That divine ecstasy, that peace, and that stillness is something He not only embodies, but also something He exudes, something He gives out freely to all who meet Him, such that no one who encounters Him is ever the same.

To capture that "touch of God" is nearly impossible in writing, for as He always says, "people need not only divine teachings, but they also need the divine touch." That "touch" is not physical, however. It does not depend upon physical contact or even physical presence. Rather, the "touch" is one in which your soul quivers in the way that a seed must as it is about to break forth through its shell and become the sprout of a large, flowering tree. The "touch" is not one of a hand to a body, but it is one of a hand to a soul. The souls, which have cried out for years and decades and lifetimes for solace, find it in His presence.

Here, in these pages, the challenge is to give not only the teachings, but also the "touch". This is a task which we have realized is impossible, for words on a page cannot make a soul quiver and burst forth into light unless these words carry within them the spirit of the Master.

Thus, in these pages you will find words that have been written or spoken by Pujya Swamiji. The spoken words have been transcribed as directly as possible from both His informal "satsang" sessions and from His more formal lectures. We pray that within these words you will find not only the teaching for your minds, but the touch for your hearts and your souls.

This book – in contrast to the earlier two editions which had two sections – is divided into three sections. The first section is a collection of articles He has written on a variety of subjects, articles which have appeared in various international magazines and yet which are applicable and valuable for all people, in all circumstances.

The second section is compiled of stories – stories He has told to audiences and followed with morals, divine lessons for how to live our lives. These stories have their origins mostly in the scriptures or occasionally in parables told by others to which Pujya Swamiji has added His own special meaning and lesson.

The third section is a potpourri of stories, quotations, letters, and poems which Pujya Swamiji has received via email over the years and which He has marked with a "save for book" and instructed me to put into a special file. They are stories and quotations which He felt should be shared with all, which could benefit all. Some of these have known authors. Most do not. Some are common and well-known, others are more obscure, but all are things which He felt should be gathered and shared, rather than simply deleted.

The title of this book is "Drops of Nectar." The nectar is a reference to the pot of the nectar of immortality, which is the essence of the story of the Maha Kumbha Mela, as the first edition was released during the Kumbha Mela of 1998. However, the true Nectar is Him. The true, divine nectar is not immortality, but rather a connection with He who bestows immortality upon us. To be immortal without Him in our lives would be to live eternally, yet alone.

For those of us who have been blessed to have Pujya Swamiji in our lives, He is that nectar and it is a great joy and honor to share "drops" of this nectar with all.

Sadhvi Bhagwati
Rishikesh, India
June, 2002

H.H. SANT SHRI RAMESHBHAI OZA
(PUJYA BHAISHRI)

ॐ A MESSAGE FROM :

PUJYA SANT RAMESHBHAI OZA (BHAISHRI)

Jai Shri Krishna !

It is by Lord Krishna's grace that you are holding such a valuable treasure in your hands. They say that a true saint is not one who is simply enlightened himself, but one who brings enlighenment to others. Pujya Swamiji is, therefore, one of the truest saints I know. His words, his life, his message and his satsang carry lakhs of people directly to God.

Pujya Swamiji is one of the rare souls whose life will have enormous impact on all of humanity — today, tomorrow and in the future. He touches and transforms all those he meets. Yet, the arms of his divine influence extend infinitely further. He is not content to only serve those who come to him. Rather, he works tirelessly, yet silently and humbly, to serve every individual creature on the planet, ranging from cows on the streets, to children in schools, to spiritual communities across the globe.

There are many saints who can give divine teachings. But the teaching is not enough. In order to truly inspire people, to touch and uplift the deepest corners of their soul, one must have the divine touch. It is that touch that Pujya Swamiji gives. So, what you have in this book is not only the word of God; it is the touch of God.

Read this book, then re-read it, then re-read it again. Let its message sink into every corner of your being. Then, if you are open enough, you will know you have been touched by God.

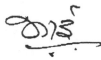

Rameshbhai Oza (Bhaishri)

ॐ ABOUT THE AUTHOR:
HIS HOLINESS PUJYA SWAMI CHIDANAND SARASWATIJI (PUJYA MUNIJI)

Spiritual and Academic Education: Touched by the hand of God at eight years old, Pujya Swamiji's youth was spent in silence, meditation and austerities high in the Himalayas. At the age of seventeen, after nine years of unbroken, intense sadhana, he returned from the forest — under the orders of his guru — and he obtained an academic education to parallel his spiritual one. Pujya Swamiji has master's degrees in Sanskrit and Philosophy as well as fluency in many languages.

The Teaching of Unity: Unity, harmony, and the belief in infinite paths to God are the foundation of Pujya Swamiji's "religion." His goal is to bring everyone closer to God, regardless of what name one uses. "If you are a Hindu, be a better Hindu. If you are a Christian, be a better Christian. If you are a Muslim, be a better Muslim. If you are a Jew, be a better Jew," he says.

In this line, he has been a leader in numerous international, inter-faith conferences and parliaments, including the Parliament of World Religions in Chicago in 1993, the Parliament of World Religions in Capetown, South Africa in 1999, and the Millennium World Peace Summit of Religious and Spiritual Leaders at the United Nations in 2000. He is also a leader of frequent Dharma Yatras across America, Canada and Europe.

Spiritual Leader and inspiration: Pujya Swamiji is the president and spiritual head of Parmarth Niketan Ashram in

Rishikesh, one of India's largest and most renowned spiritual institutions. Under his divine inspiration and leadership, Parmarth Niketan has become a sanctuary known across the globe as one filled with grace, beauty, serenity and true divine bliss. Pujya Swamiji has also increased several-fold the humanitarian activities undertaken by Parmarth Niketan. Now, the ashram is not only a spiritual haven for those who visit, but it also provides education, training, health care etc. to those in need.

He is also the founder and the spiritual head of the first Hindu Jain Temple in America. This beautiful 3-domed, masterpiece is located on the outskirts of Pittsburgh, Pennsylvania, and has paved the way for unity between Hindus and Jains across America. Pujya Swamiji is also the founder and inspiration behind many other temples in USA, Canada, Europe and Australia.

Guide to Youth: Pujya Swamiji knows the youth are our future; he is forever changing the course of that future through his profound effect on every youngster with whom he comes in contact. Children and adolescents seem to bloom like flowers under the rays of his light. Additionally, he gives pragmatic tools to help them unite in the spirit of peace, harmony and global change. Pujya Swamiji runs youth sessions and camps in USA, Europe and throughout Asia.

Ceaseless Service: "Giving is Living," is Pujya Swamiji's motto; he is always in the midst of dozens of projects, each one a noble and tenaciously dedicated effort to make the world a better place for all of humanity. He is the Founder/ Chairman of India Heritage Research Foundation (IHRF), an international, non-profit, humanitarian organization dedicated to providing education, health care, youth welfare, vocational training to the needy population. IHRF also, under the guidance and inspiration of Pujya Swamiji, is compiling the first Encyclopedia of Hinduism in history.

Awards and Recognitions: Pujya Swamiji has received dozens of awards for both his role as spiritual leader and also for his unparalleled humanitarian work. Some of the more noteworthy are as follows:

1) Mahatma Gandhi Humanitarian award, 1993, given by the Mayor of New Jersey, USA for outstanding charitable and interfaith work,

2) Hindu of the Year, 1991 by the international magazine Hinduism Today for masterminding the project of the next millennium, the Encyclopedia of Hinduism.

3) Devarishi Award, by Sandipani Vidya Niketan, under the guidance of Pujya Sant Rameshbhai Oza for promoting Indian culture and heritage across the world

4) Bhaskar Award, by Mystic India and Bharat Nirman, 1998, for Outstanding Humanitarian Service

5) Prominent Personality Award, 1999, by Lions' Club

6) Diwaliben Mohanlal Mehta Charitable Trust Award for Progress in Religion

7) Best Citizens of India Award

Further, he has been given the title of Patron of the Russian Indian Heritage Research Foundation, Moscow, and he is also a Patron of the Centre for Religious Experience in Oxford, UK.

The True Sanyasi: Pujya Swamiji seems unaffected by this incredible list of accomplishments and remains a pious child of God, owning nothing, draped in saffron robes, living a life of true renunciation. His days in Rishikesh are spent inspiring and uplifting those around him. Thousands travel from across the globe as well as from all over India, simply to sit in his presence, to receive his "darshan." To them, the journey is an inconsequential price to pay for the priceless gift of his satsang.

I have been blessed beyond words to spend the last year and a half living in Rishikesh and working with Pujya Swamiji. During this time, I have heard so many people ask, "Isn't there anything published with Swamiji's teachings? Isn't there any compilation of His ideas, His wisdom?" The answer, much to my dismay, has been "No." The absence of such a work is grievous, for the wisdom that flows forth with His every breath is worthy of being immortalized.

On this auspicious occasion of Kumbha Mela, 1998 I have taken the God-given opportunity to bring together as much "nectar of wisdom" as I could. At this sacred time, people come from every corner of the Earth to bathe in holy waters, and to imbibe of the divine nectar of immortality. Yet, what is it that truly uplifts us, that truly changes us, that truly brings our souls closer to God? For me, it has been His holy presence in my life. How to encompass, though, divine wisdom and insight in mere pages? The task is obviously impossible. Yet, while the words are a poor substitute for His presence, they carry with them the essence of His teaching and message.

I have, therefore, compiled as many of His written articles (in English) as I could find. The articles come mainly from magazines, which are published in USA and Europe for the Indian community living abroad.

In addition to the articles, there are stories, or rather parables, that I have heard Pujya Swamiji tell. I have frequently been blessed to be present at times in which someone has asked Him a question to which He did not directly respond. Rather, on these occasions, His voice took on an even more ethereal tone and his eyes drifted even more away from the Earth and toward the Heavens. He would say, "Let me tell you a story," or He would simply begin to tell it, and we all knew something extraordinary was taking place.

Then, on these occasions, when He had finished the story, He would explain —to we who are horribly ill-equipped to grasp the depth of His wisdom — what the point was. Hence, these stories have two parts: the story itself and the lesson He gave afterwards. To me, these parables and lessons are like scriptures: words spoken by God which a mere mortal has attempted to capture on paper. I beg the reader to forgive my inadequacies as a scribe. Pujya Swamiji was not as lucky as Vyasji, whose divine wisdom was captured perfectly by Lord Ganesh.

Therefore, the book has two tones. One is literary — writings which have been presented in international magazines or newspapers; the other tone, for the stories, is oral — words which have been spoken. However, while the topics of the articles (or the plots of the stories) differ, the underlying essence of Pujya Swamiji's message remains the same. His message is: go to God.

Yet, "go to God; be with God" is not only the message of His words. It is the message of His life. Every breath He takes is divine; every word He speaks is holy canon; every piece of work He does is Creation. Pujya Swamiji is a saint by title — it is His legal designation. Yet, He is more than that. He is a saint in every pore, every cell of His body. He is not only someone who sends you to God; rather, He is someone whose mere presence carries you to God. However, should one ever try to praise Him, or thank Him, or acknowledge the miraculous nature of His being, His response is always the same: a simple shrug, eyes lifted upwards, palm open to the Heavens, and the words, "It's all God's blessing."

I would like to tell a story of my own. Unlike Pujya Swamiji's, my story is not a parable meant to teach a lesson. It is a true — word for word, detail for detail — portrait of the man behind the words on the next pages.

I came to Rishikesh as a tourist. I was 25 years old, on a three month vacation from my Ph.D. program in California. How I met Pujya Swamiji and moved into Parmarth Niketan is another story, a beautiful example of God's divine plan. For now, it will suffice to say that I was there, alone, and planning to stay approximately one week. During my first two days at the ashram, on the banks of Gangaji, in Pujya Swamiji's presence, my entire being was transformed (and this transformation has not stopped yet). I was overflowing with joy, bliss and a serenity I never knew. At Ganga Aarti, the world would disappear into the blazing fire, into the depth of the voices as they sang, into the setting sun as it bounced off the waters, into the pervasive peace of Pujya Swamiji's presence.

So, the second day, I went to Pujya Swamiji. We sat in his office, alone —he a 45 year old renunciant, and me a 25 year old American girl who could barely see straight I was so filled with ecstasy. "Swamiji," I said. "I feel so incredibly blessed to be here, to have met you, to be able to spend this time on the banks of the Ganges. I feel like you have given me so much. Is there anything I can give you, anything I can do for you?"

A voice in my head that had spent 25 years being indoctrinated by the West yelled at me: "What are you saying?" After all, there we were, alone in his office. I had only known Him for two days, and I had been warned in America to "stay away from Indian gurus." I was not connected to anyone Pujya Swamiji knew; I was simply an American girl who was staying alone in the ashram for less than a week. And, most importantly, He knew that I did not have the innate Indian understanding of what a saint is and should be.

Pujya Swamiji looked at me across the table, the light streaming in through the windows, casting a brilliant halo around His head. "Anything?" he asked. The voices inside my head screamed, "No, you're crazy!" Yet, those voices remained lost inside my head; the voice that actually flowed from my heart to my mouth said, "Yes. Anything."

Pujya Swamiji paused. "You promise?" He asked, staring directly at me as though this were the most serious question in the world. I felt that I would pass out from the intensity of the hold His eyes had on me. Every word I had ever heard in my Psychology of Mind Control classes, every story I had ever read about Indian gurus surrounded by naked women and fancy cars, and every rational thought I could have were swimming in my brain, filling it with fear. "Don't promise," the voices pleaded. I could hear my mother — on the opposite end of the world — saying "Just get up and walk out."

Yet, the two feet between my brain and my heart served as a beautiful barrier, for these words did not even touch my heart. My heart was calm and still, and filled with a sense of security that I had never known. "I promise," I said, knowing that I truly would give this man — whom I had known for two days and who was old enough to be my father — anything He asked for.

The intensity of His gaze lifted and His face broke into the lightest, purest smile I had ever seen. "Okay, then, three things," He said, and even though the divine smile continued to emanate from his face, I knew that what He was going to say would change my life forever. "First," He began. "Get closer and closer to God. Every day get closer. Second, serve the world. Even if it means doing without something you want or something you think you need, give to humanity. Third, be happy. Give all your sadness, all your anger, all your bitterness to me. Give it to me and give it to Gangaji, but don't keep it in your heart. You must be happy."

I sat there, in what felt like a far-off corner of the world, in a place so beautiful it could only exist in fairy tales, across a glass table from a man who wanted nothing else from me than to be close to God. The tears streamed down my face, although they were not sad tears. They were the tears of having found truth.

I could not have told you which was brighter — the morning sun blazing its way through the window or the light streaming from His eyes. I could not have said which was purer — the red rose, still covered with morning dew, which had just opened her petals to the world, or the love pouring forth from His heart. I could not have told you who was God — the formless Almighty Lord my Jewish upbringing had said to worship, or the small, simple man, draped in saffron robes, sitting across a desk from me.

Sadhvi Bhagwati
Rishikesh, India
March, 1998

ARTICLES

ॐ SEPTEMBER 11, 2001 -
ITS MEANING, ITS MESSAGE

September 11 was a tragic day of unprecedented proportion. Never before in the history of the world had one group so blatantly, so callously, so mercilessly struck at so many thousands of innocent people.

We were in Munich, Germany on the Vishwa Dharma Prasaar Yatra, travelling first to the Caribbean, then to USA and Canada, then to UK and then to Europe, spreading the messages of peace, unity and *Vasudhaiv Kutumbakam* The (whole world is one family). In the midst of this yatra, we heard the shattering news. Times like this and acts like these almost render us speechless with sadness. It is only after the sand has settled back on the beach after the storm, that we can bend down and examine the pieces of that which was crushed in the tempest.

Those who engage in these unforgivable acts of terrorism, intimidation and violence claim that they are fighting a "jihad", a holy war. However, the term "holy war" is itself an oxymoron, a paradoxical fallacy. A war can never be holy. Only peace is holy. That which is holy is peaceful, loving, pious and compassionate. War, by its very definition, is none of these. The terrorists claim they are fighting a war in the name of God. However, there is no such thing. War – especially those acts which kill innocent people – cannot possibly be undertaken with God's consent or to win His favor. How can we – in God's name – kill His children, His creation? Could you possibly kill your sister or your brother and claim you did it for your mother or father's sake? Or that you did it in order to win your parents' appreciation? This would be absurd.

Rather than fighting a true "holy" war, the terrorists are using God's name in order to justify their own evil, violence and aggression. To me, the true "jihad" is a holy war within ourselves, a war against that which is unholy within our own hearts. This is the war which should be fought with diligence and perserverance. A holy war is not a war of killing others. A holy war is a war of annihilating our own egos, our own attachments, our own jealousies and grudges.

However, simply condemning the acts is not enough. That which happens must happen for a reason. That which happens must have a lesson inherent within it. Let us then look at what we can learn, what reassurance we can gain from this tragic event. What can take from this which will both help us grow individually as people as well as help us grow as nations and as a world?

To me, one of the most important lessons here is one of safety, one of comfort, one of complacency. So many people throughout the world (especially those living in India, or Indians who live abroad) think of everything Western as superior, as inherently "safe." If you give someone a gift and say it's "from America," their eyes will widen with anticipation. If you tell someone that a particular object you own is "from America," that automatically grants it First Class status. The idea of sending our children "to America" for studies or work is one that fills us with great pride, comfort and security. It is every parent's dream to send their children "to America," and it is every child's dream to go.

This is not simply an issue of money. It is not only that parents think their children will have a higher income in America. Rather, there is an inherent yet almost tangible feeling of safety, security and superiority about everything Western.

Additionally, from what I have seen, people living in America have a very deep sense of safety, security and invincibility. There is a sense – taught since childhood – that living under the umbrella of the American flag will guarantee not only material prosperity, but also personal comfort and safety.

And, I am not condemning this feeling. I, personally, love America and love Americans for their great openness, great honesty, eagerness and steadfastness on the path to God. And, in many ways, this feeling of security regarding the country is not misplaced. The West achieves standards of excellence which are unsurpassed anywhere else in the world. The education and professional fields are peerless.

However, none of us, regardless of where we live, regardless of where we work, regardless of where we have attained our education, is invincible and invulnerable. It is only by the grace of God that we wake from our sleep each day. It is only by the grace of God that each of the billions of neurons in our brain continue to function properly, allowing us to breathe and our hearts to beat. It is only by the grace of God that our legs move when we think "move" and that our ears can process the sounds we hear. It is only His grace that the thousands and thousands of blood vessels in our body, continue to carry blood safely to and from the heart, without rupturing along the way.

We must take this opportunity – as tragically given as it is – to turn back to God, for He is the only true protector. No insurance policy could have protected those thousands of poor, innocent people working in the high reaches of the WTC on September 11. No matter how good the policy or how high the premium, once that tragic moment came it was only a matter of them and God. It is only our Divine Insurance Policy in whom we can have total trust. It is only the Divine Insurance Policy who truly renders us safe and protected. Thus, let us turn back to Him and realize that we are simply in His hands and that it is only by His will and His grace that we continue to exist and to prosper.

Another important realization is that the tragedy struck the top CEOs as quickly and mercilessly as it struck the lowly mail deliverers or the indigent cleaning people and window washers. The tragedy struck those with Ph.Ds from Harvard in the same swoop with those who dropped out of high school. It struck those living in the posh suburbs of Long Island as ruthlessly as it struck those sharing cramped apartments in Soho.

This does not mean, of course, that there is no benefit to advanced degrees or good jobs. It is wonderful to be successful. I always advise my youth to study, study and study so they will succeed. However, it means that we must see these achievements for what they can really give us –

comfort, ease and the ability to perform up to our potential. However, they cannot provide us with safety, security or immortality. It is only by turning to Him, by dedicating our hearts and our lives to Him (regardless of our profession) that we are truly safe and truly secure, not just our bodies but our souls.

Yes, the perpetrators should be punished. Yes, they should be brought to justice in whatever way possible. Yes, we must show the world that these sorts of crimes will not be tolerated. However, is war the answer? Is dropping bombs on a country full of innocent, impoverished people the answer? Do we need to sacrifice more innocent lives in order to avenge the death of innocents? Will an "eye for an eye" make us a better world, or will it make us all blind?

The violence perpetrated against New York and Washington, as well as the innumerable acts of terrorism throughout history, are acts of ignorance and hatred. They are acts of people who are trained to think of "us versus them." They are acts of those who are taught to see people according to color, religion and nationality. These are all veils of ignorance, veils of illusion. The solution cannot be to continue fighting from behind borders and beneath banners of religion, nationality, color or creed. The solution can only come by breaking these borders, by breaking these boundaries and by throwing away these banners.

The answer cannot come by the civilized, educated, peaceful nations of the world lowering themselves to the level of the ignorant. Rather, the wise ones must educate the others. We must continue to spread the messages of *Vasudhaiv Kutumbakam* (the whole world is one family).

We must continue to pray *"Sarve bhavantu sukhinah, sarve santu niramayah, sarve bhadrani pash-yantu, ma kashchid dukhabhagbhavet,"* (May all beings be happy. May all beings be healthy. May all see the divinity in everything. May there be no unhappiness or sorrow). For, if we, too, start to pray only *"Hindavah bhavantu sukhinah, Hindavah santu niramayah..."* (May Hindus be happy. May Hindus be healthy...) or *"Americaha bhavantu sukhinah, Americaha santu niramayaha".* (May Americans be happy. May Americans be healthy...), then we will fall into the same well of despair as those who have committed these horrendous acts.

In the months since this tragedy, we have seen more bloodshed, we have seen vengeance, we have seen more and more killing across the world along the lines of "religion." Whether it is in Afganistan, in Israel, in India or in other nations of the world, the violence is only increasing. We may squash one rebellious regime only to see another popping up in its place. We arrest, convict or kill one villainous leader only to see another rising to power in his place.

The answer, therefore, cannot come from wildly swinging the bats of our "punishment" at terrorists, at tyrannical leaders, or at regimes dedicated to genocide. For every step we take on the path to "eradicating" the leaders and regimes that exist, it seems that another two are born in their place.

This does not mean we should be lenient. This does not mean we should give up in defeat. Yes, the murderous, oppressive leaders must be removed from power. Yes, the terrorists must be brought to justice. Yes, those governmental systems which allow and encourage violence must be dealt with strictly and properly.

However, we must not think that that is enough. It is not enough. The change must come from the inside. Frequently I hear parents tell stories of their teenage daughters who have been strictly forbidden from dating, who have been punished time and again for talking endlessly on the phone with boys, who have been sternly prohibited from being alone with a boy. These girls appear to concede in the face of their parents' severity, and they appear to be remorseful and repentant as the punishment is issued. However, the parents continue to find that that the girls are escaping through their windows at night, or are concocting stories of study groups with girlfriends, while they are at the movies with their sweetheart.

Yes, the parents must continue to act authoritatively. They must not give up and allow their girls boundless freedom simply because the girls are disobeying. They must continue to punish when rules are broken, and they must continue to enact rules that will prevent further disobedience.

However, once the parents realize that the girls are merely acquiescing on the surface -- to avoid the same lecture, punishment or castigation -- they must look deeper into why the girls are engaging in this rebellious behavior.

The point here is not about disciplining teenage girls or about rules for dating. The point is that it is never enough to simply censure, punish or seek revenge. That does not change the nature of the criminal and does not prevent future aggressive, rebellious acts.

We must look deeper than treaties, deeper than squashing one regime after another, deeper than the death penalty for terrorists. We must look to the nature of the crime and the nature of the criminal if we want to effect a lasting change.

Let us put our global resources -- money, time, energy -- into not only punishing those who have committed these atrocious acts, but into creating a world system in which these acts cannot exist, into creating a world system in which terrorism is unheard of, and in which we live side by side in peace.

That is truly the task at hand. It is a task which I believe is as worthy of global resources as the task of hunting down one man hiding in the mountainous caves of Afghanistan or Pakistan.

Lastly, God has given us an important lesson in this tragedy: life is so short. We don't know when or how our end will come. Every moment is a gift. No matter how high we build our towers of prosperity, we never know when they can come crashing down. Therefore, why not live peacefully, why not live every moment in love, in harmony, in joy? Who knows if this moment will be our last?

Let us take a new pledge today, in the fertile ground of the rubble. Let us vow to live our lives as precious gifts, to come together as sister and brother, to forgive and forget our grievances and our grudges, and to join hands together in rebuilding the towers. But let these new towers be not only towers of trade and towers of wealth, but let them be towers of love, towers of unity, towers of brotherhood, towers of peace. Let these new, divine towers reach unprecedented heights, soaring toward the Divine, Infinite Abode of the Lord.

We, on the holy banks of Mother Ganga, in the lap of the sacred Himalayas, offer our deepest prayers that the departed souls may rest in peace, and that those who are shattered, broken and bereaved by this tragedy may find solace and serenity.

Lastly, we pray for those who have committed this atrocious act and for all those who have plans or desires to commit a similar act — we pray that God may bestow wisdom and compassion upon them, so that they can see the folly of their ways and transform themselves.

We pray for peace to the Heavens, peace to the Earth, peace to all the humans, all the animals, all the plants and peace for every being in the universe.

Om Shantih Shantih Shantih

# VEGETARIANISM:
A NEW LIGHT, A NEW LIFE

"Teaching a child not to step on a caterpillar is as valuable to the child as it is to the caterpillar."

We make many choices in our lives without ever questioning "why?" Choices like what religion we believe in, what our values are, what we eat... Perhaps we simply continue to live in the way we were raised; perhaps we automatically adopt our parents' choices. Or, perhaps we rebel against how we were raised: our parents made one choice, so we will make the opposite. In either case, we rarely take the time to truly see why we are living the way we do.

In this article, I want to take the opportunity to see why we — as Hindus — live as vegetarians. I want to talk about the deep meanings behind this choice we make each time we put food in our bodies.

I hear so many youth tell me, "But my parents can't even give me a good reason to be vegetarian. They just say that the cow is holy, but if I don't believe the cow is holy then why can't I eat hamburgers?"

The importance of vegetarianism far transcends a belief that the cow is holy. In fact, although the tenet of vegetarianism is as true as it was thousands of years ago, the reasons "why" have changed slightly. Some of the meanings and reasons are the same today as when our scriptures were written thousands of years ago. However, many of the reasons are directly related to the world we live in now. While vegetarianism has always been a correct "moral" and "spiritual" choice, today it is more than that.

Today, it is an imperative choice for anyone who is concerned about the welfare of Mother Earth and all the people who live here. Today, it is not only a religious decision. Rather, it is the only way we can hope to eliminate hunger, thirst, rainforest destruction and the loss of precious resources. It is, in short, the most important thing that each man, woman and child can do every day to demonstrate care for the earth and care for humanity.

Spiritual/Religious Aspects of Vegetarianism

One of the most important guiding principles of a moral life is *ahimsaa*, or non-violence. There is hardly anything more violent than taking the life of another for our mere enjoyment. It would be one thing if we were stranded in the jungle, starving to death, and we needed the food to survive. But, we live in a world where we can get all our calories, all our vitamins and minerals in other, tastier, less expensive and less violent ways. Hence, to continue to kill the animals is simply to fulfill our desires, our pleasures. It is simply selfish gratification at the incredible pain of another.

Perhaps more violent than their day of death is the numerous days of their lives. The animals raised for consumption are a distinctly different species from the animals raised as pets, or raised for their byproducts (e.g. milk from a cow). Veal is a poignant, yet compelling example. This meat is considered a rare delicacy by people across the world. "Tender veal cutlets" are frequently the most expensive item on a menu. Yet, when we look at the way in which these animals become so tender, we realize that the true price of this dish is far more than the what the restaurant charges.

Veal is the meat from baby cows who are separated from their mothers immediately at birth. Cows, as milk-giving/breast-feeding mammals have very strong maternal instincts. It is not a simple coincidence that Hindus worship the cow as mother. A mother cow will keep her calf next to her long after he is born, looking after him, protecting him, teaching him to fend for himself. But, these baby cows are wrested from their new mothers. I have heard from people who have visited these places that — contrary to what people will tell you — the mother and baby cows cry in agony for hours after being separated.

But, it is essential that the babies do not develop any muscle. And if they stand near their mothers, their legs will develop muscle. And muscle is hard; fat is soft and juicy. Fat is tender. The difficulty is that if one uses one's limbs at all, one develops muscle. So, the only way to prevent muscle is to prevent use of the limbs. So, these newborn baby cows, screaming for the warmth of their mother's breast, are buried in the sand or locked into restraining boxes. Their entire bodies up to the neck are buried. If you have ever tried to move a foot or a hand that is buried in the sand, you will know that it is impossible. Especially if you are a baby with no muscle. They are fed copious amounts of food directly into their mouths, more than babies should theoretically eat, so they will become fat quickly. However, they are never removed from the confines of the sand or the restraining box. And this lasts not one day, not one week, but many months, until they are killed and sold as "tender veal cutlets." So, what is the real price of this dish?

Now, let's look at chickens. Many people (especially in the West) say they are a vegetarian, but they still eat chicken. The life of a chicken is only scarcely better than the life of the baby cows. They are put in crates, which are piled high on top of each other. In this way, not only are they denied space to move, let alone roam around, but when one chicken goes to the bathroom, it falls through the crates onto the chickens below. The crates are never cleaned and the chickens never see the sunlight; the light from the artificial bulbs is enough to keep them functioning.

Chickens — like humans — have natural territory and space needs. Yet, these are unmet in chicken "farms." Rather, these animals are packed together as closely as possible, such that frequently they can not even move. To have a true understanding of these conditions, picture yourself in an elevator, which is so crowded that you can not even turn around, let alone move. Picture as well, that all the people in the elevator are confused and scared. They do not realize there is no way out. So they cry and bite and kick, in a true frenzy, attempting free themselves from this claustrophobic terror. Next, imagine that the elevator is tilted, on a slant, so that everyone falls to one side, and it is nearly impossible to move back "up." In this elevator, the ceiling is so low that your head is pushed down to your shoulders in order to stand. There is no way to straighten your neck. And you are all barefoot on a wire floor that pokes and cuts your feet — ever so sensitive for you are probably only a few months old. Finally, imagine that this terror does not end when someone comes to open the door at the "lobby" floor. Rather, it is your life. Every minute of every day, until you are fried up and served for dinner, with a side of mashed potatoes.

It would be one thing if we were stranded in the jungle, starving to death, and we needed the food to survive. But, we live in a world where we can get all our calories, all our vitamins and minerals in other, tastier, less expensive and less violent ways. Hence, to continue to kill the animals is simply to fulfill our desires, our pleasures. There is no need or utility in it. It is simply selfish gratification at the incredible pain of another.

Integrity and Honesty

How many of us consider ourselves honest people? How many of us can say that we do not tell lies? We would very much like to believe that we are righteous, honest people and that we are passing these values onto our children. Well, if we eat meat, we can not say that we do not tell lies. In fact, our life is a lie. Here is why: if we wanted to be honest and still eat meat, we would have to go outside, chase down a live cow, and bite right into it. Or we would have to go to one of those chicken "farms," take the animal while it was still alive, tear its head off, pull out its feathers and eat it raw. Of course, we do not do that. Instead, we order a hamburger. We can not even call it what it is, let alone kill it ourselves. So, we call it beef, instead of cow. We call it pork instead of pig. We call it poultry instead of chicken. And we eat it packaged in neat, nice ways that allow us to forget what we are eating.

How many people stop and think that the thing between the tomato and the bread on a hamburger used to be a living, breathing creature? That it was someone's child?

How many of us would eat our cats or dogs between a piece of tomato and a slice of bread? We wouldn't. And that is why it is a lie. We can not even admit to ourselves what we are doing. How then, can we consider ourselves honest people if we are lying every time we eat? And these are not lies that only cause misunderstanding; these are not "little white lies." These are lies that are killing our planet, our animals and ourselves.

The Taste of Fear

Additionally, eating meat is violent not only to the animal whose life we are wresting from it, but it is also violent to ourselves and our planet. The violence manifests in other, more subtle ways. When animals (humans included) are threatened, we secrete large amounts of hormones. These numerous hormones are frequently referred to as adrenaline. Their purpose is to prepare our body to fight, to save our lives. Have you ever noticed that when you get scared, a lot of things happen inside you? Your heart beats fast, your digestion stops, your palms sweat and your physical impulses become very good and sharp. These are the result of the hormones. And they prepare us to either fight or run away. Thus, they are sometimes called the "fight or flight" hormones.

When an animal is about to be killed, its body is flooded with these stress hormones which remain in the animals' tissues. So, when we eat those tissues, we are ingesting those hormones (which are the same as our own bodies make). Thus, our own bodies become flooded with these "fight or flight" chemicals, making us even more prone to simple survival instincts.

Our world is becoming more violent each day. More and more people are simply out to get ahead, to protect themselves, even at the sake of others. These are the same characteristics that adrenaline and the other stress hormones prepare our bodies for. Hence, is it not possible, that the increase in these characteristics world wide, is directly a result of our increase in meat consumption, and the subsequent ingestion of stress hormones? I think it is.

So, if we truly want to reduce the violence, the hate in this world, perhaps we should stop flooding our bodies with hormones that create stress and the readiness to fight, to save our own lives at the sake of another's. Perhaps, if we treat this temple that is our bodies as a temple it will behave and think like a temple. When we treat it like a battleground, how can we wonder that it acts like a battleground?

Vegetarianism and Ecology

Aside from all the compelling moral and spiritual reasons, one can now say that vegetarianism is the only responsible choice in terms of waste and ecology. The natural resources of our planet are diminishing at terrifying rates. More than a third of the world goes to bed hungry each night. And we wonder what we can do. Being a vegetarian addresses almost each and every ecological issue.

Are you concerned about **world hunger**? Let me give you some facts.

*   It takes 16 pounds of wheat to produce one pound of meat. This wheat is fed to the cows who are later killed to make beef. However, it takes only 1 pound of wheat to produce one pound of bread. So, if we used our wheat

to produce bread rather than feed it to cows in order to make hamburgers, we could feed 16 times as many people.

- One acre of land can grow 40,000 pounds of potatoes. That same acre, can provide less than 250 pounds of beef if it is used to grow cattle-feed.

- If Westerners reduced their intake of meat by only 10% (it means they would still eat 90% as much meat as they do now), we could feed every one of the 50,000 people who die of starvation every day.

- Every day, 40,000 children starve to death. Every day the US produces enough grain to provide EVERY person on Earth with 2 loaves of bread

- Today, already 840 million go hungry every year.

- We could feed 10 billion people a year if we were all vegetarian. This is more than human population. There is no need for ANYONE to go hungry in the world – the only reason is the selfishness of the choices we make.

Are you concerned about **destruction of the rainforests** and other precious land? Well,

- A great deal of the livestock are raised on forest land. It is estimated that for every hamburger, 55 square feet of rainforest land is destroyed.

- Additionally for this one hamburger, 500 pounds of Carbon Dioxide (one of the main gases leading to the global warming problem) are released into the air.

- Since 1967, one acre of American forest has been destroyed every five seconds, in order to become "grazing land" for the animals that will become dinner.

If the present trend continues, the country that was seen as the "land of plenty" will be completely stripped bare of all its forests in 50 years. Do not let Europe make the same mistake.

Are you concerned about **poverty** in the world?

- A pound of protein from meat costs $15.40, but a pound of protein from wheat costs $1.50.

- So, meat costs 10 times as much for the same nutritional value.

- Could we not use that money for such better causes? Is there no more important use for that money than to kill animals?

Are you worried about our rapidly diminishing **energy** resources?

- The world's petroleum resources would last only 13 years on a meat-based diet, but 260 years on a vegetarian diet.

Are you aware of the need to **conserve water**?

- The production of 1 pound of beef takes 2500 gallons of water.

- The production of 1 pound of bread takes 25 gallons of water

- So, we would waste 100 times less water if we ate wheat instead of meat.

Health issues

I am not going to use this space to tell you about all the health reasons to eat a vegetarian diet. Every medical text, every health book, in every bookstore or library talks about the undeniable link between high-fat diets and heart disease or cancer. It is well known that people who eat meat based diets have anywhere from 2 to 20 times higher rates of death from heart disease and cancer than vegetarians.

A recent British study found that vegetarians had a 40% lower risk of cancer and a 20% lower risk of death from any cause than meat eaters.

In fact, Dr. Dean Ornish, M.D. a cardiac specialist in California, USA is the first allopathic doctor ever to be able to "cure" heart disease. Others have slowed the process but never before has it been truly cured. His "cure" consists of a pure vegetarian diet, yoga and meditation.

A health issue less frequently discussed is the antibiotics factor. The animals are loaded up with antibiotics in order to prevent the diseases that their poor treatment causes. The environments are so unsanitary that the animals have great risk of developing infections. So, antibiotics are fed to them in great quantity. When we eat the animals, we ingest the antibiotics as well.

However, bacteria are resilient. They develop resistance/immunity to antibiotics, whether we take it or simply eat the meat of an animal who has taken it. So, then when we, ourselves, are sick and actually need the antibiotics, they do not work. This is because our bodies have already developed resistances to them, through so many years of ingesting them through meat.

Each year more and more antibiotics become futile and powerless; each year there are more and more resistant strains of bacterial infections. Many people believe that the reason for this is that as we consume low doses for so many years through our consumption of meat, the bacteria all have a chance to mutate and become resistant.

Another issue has to do with hormones. The animals are fed large doses of hormones to make fatter, bigger, and "juicier." There is substantial evidence that over-secretion of hormones within our own bodies leads to disease. For example, over secretion of adrenaline and the stress hormones can lead to heart disease. Over secretion of estrogen has been associated with cancer in women. Yet, when we eat the meat, it's the same hormones.

We are not only eating meat, but we are eating hormones that our bodies don't need and that may be putting our lives and health in jeopardy.

Conclusion

Across the industrialized world, everyone is talking about what we can do to save the planet. Ecological conservation has become a household word. There are thousands of programs dedicated to feeding the millions of starving children. Yet, while we may talk about wanting to save the planet or feed the hungry, these words are empty if our actions show blatant disregard. We may not be able to carry crates of food to the deserts of Africa. We may not be able to re-plant every tree that has been cut down in the forest. But, we can refuse to allow it to continue. We can refuse to partake of the cruelty. We can strive to make, at least our lives and our actions pure and divine.

Instead of a token donation to a hunger campaign or to an environmental organization, let us make our every day, every meal, one that protects not only our own health, but the health of our planet and the health of every person on it.

ॐ REBIRTH AND REINCARNATION

1.   Rebirth is the philosophy of the Hindu religion. Does any other religion advocate the same philosophy?
Sikhism, Jainism and Buddhism also adhere to the philosophy of rebirth.

2.   What is the meaning of rebirth. What relevance does it have to the common man?
The literal meaning of rebirth is the act of the soul casting off the body in which it had lived and inhabiting a new body, one which will be conducive to its evolution.

This is incredibly significant for people, for the undeniable implication is that our "lives" are not merely limited to the 50 or 60 or even 80 years we spend in this current body, but rather we will live again and again. Intricately connected to the philosophy of rebirth is the philosophy of karma, for it is our karma which determines the body that our soul will inhabit next. Our karma determines both the positive and the negative situations in which our soul will find itself in the future. Thus, if we cause pain to others in this life, it is likely that we will experience pain, both in this birth and in the future.

Relevance of Rebirth

The belief in this philosophy serves several purposes for people. First, it ensures that we live our lives honestly, compassionately and purely. If we fully understand that our present actions determine our future circumstances, then we will act with discretion, love, peace and generosity. In the same way that people do not speed in their car when there is a policeman present, for fear of receiving a ticket, so we will not speed (or otherwise break the laws) in our lives when we realize that every action is being recorded.

However, the belief in this philosophy also provides hope to people. We see that this life is not our only chance. If someone has lived a life of greed, of lust, of anger and of *adharma* and if he does NOT adhere to the philosophy of rebirth, then he would feel hopeless and fated to an eternity of "Hell." On the other hand, rebirth offers him another chance. The laws of rebirth and karma say, "your future begins right now. Change yourself today so that your future may be bright."

3.   *What is the reasoning and purpose behind rebirth?*

There are several purposes to rebirth. The **first purpose** lies in the realization that **as humans we are weak.** We succumb to temptation, to desire and to our emotions. Rebirth offers us a vision of life as a continuation from low to high, from impure to pure, and from human to divine. The law of rebirth allows us to both accept our "humanness" graciously without feeling damned to a life in Hell, while simultaneously striving to live our lives in a way that will ensure a positive tomorrow.

Second, the purpose of rebirth is to show people the **inevitable repercussions of our actions.** If you play "hide and seek" with a small child, she will frequently "hide" right in the middle of the room, closing her eyes in the belief that since she cannot see you, you must also not be able to see her. People also live like this, assuming that just because they claim not to "believe" in the law of karma that it doesn't affect them. Yet, although our eyes may be closed, the Almighty God can still see us, and His law of karma "catches" us regardless of where we are.

There is a beautiful story in which a guru is deciding to which of his three disciples he should leave his large ashram and estate. To each he gives an apple and instructs his disciples to go, eat the apple where no one can see them, and then to return. He who returns first, having successfully completed the task, will receive the ashram.

So, 2 hours later, the first disciple runs back, breathless. He says, "Oh Guruji, am I the first back? I have climbed to the top of the highest mountain. It was so high that even animals cannot live there. There, on the peak of the highest mountain, out of sight of all humans and animals, I ate the apple." The Guru just nods his head.

Later that evening the second disciple returns. He says, "Guruji, I went into a cave deep in the ground. Down deep below the surface of the Earth, in the darkness of the cave, I ate the apple. Not even a worm could see me, as I was so deep that not even a ray of light could penetrate." The Guru nodded.

The night passed and the third disciple did not return. Finally, the following afternoon, more than 24 hours after the Guru had given the assignment, the third disciple walked in, slowly, with his head hanging low. He looked up shamefully at the Guru and placed the apple back into the Guru's hands. He said, "My revered Guruji, I have failed in my task. I climbed to the highest mountain, I descended into the depths of the Earth. I went into open fields and into closed, constricted burrows. However, there was nowhere I could eat my apple, for regardless of where I was, I could see the eyes of the Lord watching me." The Guru smiled at his disciple and said, "My child, you are the one who shall inherit my ashram, for only you know the omniscience and omnipresence of God. He can see in the darkest darkness. He can see to the highest peak. He can see near and far. He can see even that to which we, ourselves, our blind."

So, in the same way, there is no way we can escape the eyes of karma or the law of rebirth. Thus, through these laws, God has given us both a never-ending, continuous chance of self-improvement and also an inescapable equation by which we always reap what we sow.

Third, another important point of rebirth is to fulfil unfulfilled desires. As long as we have desires for anything other than God, we cannot attain liberation. In fact, liberation is the freedom from all desires. Thus, until our mind becomes desireless, we will continue to engage ourselves in actions to fulfil these desires. These actions are what lead to karma – both good and bad – and thus bind us in the chains of birth and death. Thus, through rebirth we continue to live until have realized that God is the thing worth desiring. Then, falling in surrender at His holy feet, we begin the path toward desirelessness and liberation.

Thus, the most important purpose and reason of rebirth is to attain liberation, to become one with God. People can go astray in one life. People can choose paths of passion instead of piety, paths of decadence instead of discrimination, and paths of hedonism instead of honor. Yet, God wants us all to come to Him. That is the purpose of human birth. So, He gives us more chances. We keep coming back until we learn the lessons of this human birth and until we transcend the limitations and temptations of the flesh. Thus, we must realize that everything we do which is not conducive to the path of God realization, is simply an obstacle we are putting in our own way. Every act we commit which is not honest, divine and pure is simply one more stumbling block we put on our path. It is simply one more hurdle we will have to cross, if not this life then next life.

4.   We know about the ten incarnations of Lord VISHNU. In which way does God descend on earth? Does he take birth in the same way as that of the common man or through some other way?
God is God, so He can manifest in any way. He can manifest in human forms or in non-human forms. He is not limited in any way. The rules of man do not apply to God. All of His manifestations are divine.

5.   How many times can a soul take birth. Can a soul say that's enough, now I do not want to be reborn birth. Is this request ever accepted?
A soul will come to Earth in human form as many times as are necessary to attain the final state of liberation. The faster one progresses, the fewer births that are necessary. Yes, a soul can certainly decide that this is enough and

that it does not want to be reborn. However, simply wanting liberation is not enough. One must work for it. This is the point of sadhana, of seva, of japa, of meditation, of yoga. Through these ways, the soul sheds layer after layer of illusion, ignorance, attachment and desire. Once the layers have all been shed, once the soul realizes its true, divine nature, then rebirth is not necessary. Through these disciplines one can break the cycle of birth and death.

Attaining liberation is not merely due to a "request." Sure, of course, one can request it, but that request is not enough. Rather than just giving us liberation as per request, God gives us the light by which we can see the path toward Him. He gives us the light of discrimination, the light of wisdom, and the light of truth by which we can find our way.

Thus, we cannot simply say, "I want liberation" and then continue to accrue karma which will bind us. All actions which are not laid at His holy feet – whether they are good actions or bad actions – result in karma. In order to completely break the chain of karma, we must lay our entire lives – every thought, every action, every word, and every desire – at His holy feet, realizing that He is the doer and we are merely the vessel through which He does.

In the Bhagwat Gita, Bhagwan Krishna says:

Yat karosi yad asnasi, yaj juhosi dadasi yat
Yat tapasyasi kaunteya, tat kurusva mad-arpanam.
Subhasubha-phalair evam moksyase karmabandhanaih
Sannyasa-yoga-yuktatma vimukto mam upaisyasi

This means, "Whatever you do, whatever you eat, whatever you give, and whatever sadhana and tapasa you perform, do everything as an offering to Me. In this way you will be freed from the bondage of karma and from the results of karma in your life. Through this renunciation of everything unto me, you will be free of all bondage and you will become united with Me."

Further, it is only through becoming desireless that we can stop accruing karma and attain salvation. Yet, in order to become desireless we must practice sadhana to realize God. A child will be very attached to his toys and will desire more toys. However, by the time he is an adult, he will no longer be interested in these toys, "There are more important things than toys," he will say. If you gave him a choice between diamonds and toy trucks, he would of course choose the diamonds. Similarly, we must reach a state where God is the diamond and all else are worthless toys.

When we perform yagna we say, "Idam Agnaye, swaha, idam agnaye, idam na mama." This means, "not for me, but for You, God." This must be our attitude not only in havan ceremonies, but also in every action of our life. Everything must be done as an offering to Him.

6. The next birth for a saint like you will be progressive and important like this birth. Do you know which will be your next birth?

For me personally, I am not concerned about where I take birth. I want only to continue to serve God through service to His children. The point of rebirth is not to be concerned with the when, where and how, but rather to make the Here and Now your Heaven! Liberation can take place now, if only we will work for it.

With the blessings of God and the grace of God, every moment of every day can be Liberation. In a rat race, you are always a rat. Even if you win the race, you are still a rat. The point of life is to live with Grace, not in a race. Yes, we must perform our duties. Yes, we must try to succeed in whatever way we are able. But, we must live in Grace, not in a Rat Race! That is the point of a divine life.

We should take the divine life of bhakta Prahlad as an example. Lord Vishnu offered him anything. What did he ask for? What boon did he request from God? He said, "Regardless of where I take birth, regardless of what form I come in – be it a scorpion, an insect, a tree, an animal or a man – the form and the place and the circumstances are irrelevant to me. I only ask that, in whatever form I take future births, please bestow upon me the blessing of undying devotion for Your holy feet." The only thing he wanted was to live his life with the divine nectar of bhakti filling every pore of his body. He wanted to be completely saturated with love for God. This is the point of life.

7. If someone lives a virtuous life and achieves nirvana, does that mean there is no rebirth for him?

Yes, if one achieves nirvana, then that is the goal of human birth and one is liberated from the cycle of birth and death. However, saints may choose to return to the Earth, although they don't have to, in order to ease the pain of those who are living. Yet, the difference between the liberated souls and those who are still bound by the laws of karma is like the difference between the prisoner and the jailer. Both live within the confines of the jail. However, where the prisoner must live according to the rules of the jail and his every movement is restricted, the jailer is free to move about as he wishes. He is not subject to the rules and no one is monitoring his movements. Further, while the prisoner must stay in the jail until his term is up, the warden is free to leave – either temporarily or even to give up his position as jail warden.

Similarly, the enlightened soul is on Earth, knowingly and by choice, in order to help others attain liberation. He is free and not bound.

8. Can a person really have any knowledge of a previous birth? If so is this knowledge beneficial or does it have disadvantages?

Usually people cannot remember previous births. One must perform great sadhana or go to the saints or special jyotishi (expert astrologer) to learn about their previous births. It is usually not advantageous to know, which is why the Divine Plan does not give us easy access to that information. We have enough trouble trying to navigate through one life, with one husband or wife, one mother, one father, one job, etc. Imagine if we immediately recognized others as our previous parents or spouses or vicious enemies? It would be impossible to remain neutral and unbiased.

Imagine that a man is married to a woman with whom he is not deeply in love. Certainly he loves her but not passionately or deeply. However, due to his duties, he stays married and lives an upright life. Now, imagine that one day he sees a very old woman in the grocery store and immediately recognizes her as his beloved from an earlier birth. He would have great difficulty not leaving his wife and family for an old woman whom he lusted for passionately in an earlier life!

Or, imagine that an upstanding young man and a young woman fall in love. The man goes to the woman's parents to request her hand in marriage, and the girl's father immediately recognizes the boy as an enemy from an earlier life. He would never allow his daughter to marry the man, although perhaps through the last few lives the man had gone from being a rascal to being a righteous young man.

So, in this way our lives would be quite difficult if we remembered our earlier births. Additionally, people talk about remembering our "last life," but how many lives do we want to remember? One, three, ten, fifty? Where would we stop? Eventually, we would be living in a situation where many people we met had played some role in an earlier birth, thus preventing us from treating them fairly and dispassionately in this birth.

9.   Why should the soul take birth on earth only? After leaving the human body, can a soul be born in any other form?

When we realize the purpose of rebirth, then it becomes clear as to why the Earth is the best-suited place and why the human body is the best-suited medium. The purpose, as we have discussed, is to work through previous karmas, to become desireless (through either fulfilment of the desires or through sadhana to eradicate the desires), and to attain God realization. The human body – with its intellect, compassion, consciousness, yearning, understanding and wisdom – is the most conducive to attain God realization. As an animal, our lives would be spent solely in eating, sleeping, protecting ourselves and reproducing. There is not time or ability for sadhana. Similarly for plants and other species – the consciousness is there in terms of ability to feel pain and to reproduce, but there is not a well developed enough sense to search for something higher.

However, occasionally, due to the performance of truly evil deeds and the accumulation of significant negative karma, a soul will have to come to Earth in the form of an insect or lower life form. However, as soon as the lessons are learned in that life form, then again the soul can come in the form of a human, in order to continue its progression toward God realization.

10. How many times does a soul have to take birth? Does the same soul always take birth on Earth? When he is born, does he look the same each time?

First of all, the soul never actually takes birth. Rather, the soul inhabits human bodies in order to come to Earth, the Karma Bhoomi (land of karma) so that it can engage itself in actions which will lead to its liberation. The individual soul – which is intricately connected to the mind, the senses and the desires — comes to the Earth in those situations which will be most conducive to working through past karmas, to enabling the mind to become pure and desireless, and to helping it attain salvation.

People frequently become confused that it is the soul which must work through karma or the soul which has desires. No, the soul is pure, divine and complete. Rather, it is the mind, the senses, the pranas, the desires, the sanskaras and the tendencies which form the subtle body and travel with the soul from one gross body to the next gross body and which obscure the true, divine perfection of the soul.

It is like a perfect reflection of the sun (the individual soul as reflection of the Supreme Reality) which becomes distorted and murky due to the dirt and waves in the water in which it is being reflected (the mind and the senses). The reflection (the soul) is perfect. It is only the vehicles of reflection (the mind and senses) which are turbulent and murky, thus making the reflection itself seem less than clear. Once the water becomes clear and calm, the sun will reflect perfectly. Similarly, once the mind and the senses become calm and clear, through sadhana, through association with the saints, through good work, then the individual soul can manifest perfectly and attain liberation.

11.   If we have good parents, brothers, sisters, friends and gurus, how can we have the same relatives and friends in the next life. Does a soul have any right to select his family and friends?

There are two important points. Yes, on the one hand we can hope to be with certain people again in our next life. The only way to do this is through prayer. It is not a matter of the soul having a "right" to choose. But, rather, if someone prays with great sincerity, purity and devotion God can answer the prayer.

However, the other important point is that the purpose of life is NOT to become so attached to our family and friends that we are already worried about not being with them in our next birth. We have a hard enough time living together in this life! So many times we cannot even get along with our family members in this life; we must focus on loving and caring for each other NOW, rather than be concerned about whether we will be together in the future.

Also, when a soul departs from the body, the soul continues its journey toward God realization. The scriptures caution us against thwarting the progress of other souls. By begging to stay together with someone, we are inhibiting their own progress and path.

Thus, let us instead concentrate on loving those we are with now. Let us care for all those who come into our path. Let us pray to move forward with each birth, and let us not be so attached that we sacrifice our own or someone else's spiritual growth in order to simply stay together.

12.   Does the karma of this life become useful in the next life? If the present life is happy, does that mean the soul has done good deeds? On the contrary, if this life is full of unhappiness, does that mean the soul is suffering from his own misdeeds of his last birth? Can you please explain the law of karma?

Yes, the karma of this life is extremely relevant to our next life. However, the equation is not as simple as just good deeds in one life lead to happiness in the next, or bad deeds lead to unhappiness. First of all, karma can take place immediately; it does not necessarily wait until the next birth. We always reap that which we sow. Therefore, performing good deeds with a selfless motive will definitely lead to positive karma, both in this life AND in future lives.

However, there are a few important points. First of all, motivation is important. We must perform our duties with no motivation other than to do God's will purely and selflessly. If we simply do good deeds so that we will reap good karma (e.g. going to temple in order to pass an exam, or being respectful to your mother so that she will raise your allowance) then we do not really get the long-term benefits. Rather, we must do good deeds because it is the right thing to do. We must perform right action because that is what will lead us to God. We must not concern ourselves with the immediate fruits or results.

Second, it is important to realize that that which may seem to be negative is not necessarily so. For example if a young, pure, innocent boy dies at the age of ten, people immediately question, "what horrible sin did he commit in a past birth in order to account for the tragedy in this one?" Perhaps the death was due to negative karma. However, perhaps he had come very close to liberation in a past birth and only had a few karmas to work through before his soul was ready for salvation. These karmas may have been quickly resolved during only ten years and thus, the soul is free to be liberated. So, rather than being a tragedy, the early death is a blessing.

13. *Can a great soul take birth again to finish his life's work. Are there any such examples. Or two lovers failed to live together in this life, if they shorten their lives by committing suicide, will they then be together in their next life?*

Yes, of course, souls can come back to finish their work. That is why they come back – because their work of attaining divine liberation is not completed. There are many examples through history of proven cases of reincarnation. In fact, when I was young, doing sadhana in the Himalayan jungle, I met several people (including very small children) who told me about their path births, even down to the smallest detail of the home in which they lived and their previous families. They explained the circumstances of their death and how their work was thwarted by death. These details of their lives have been confirmed through independent sources.

However, to commit suicide in the hope that in next life our wishes will be fulfilled is a grave mistake. This is true regardless of what our wishes are, whether they are wishes to be with a particular boy or girl or whether they are wishes to succeed in a particular arena. Suicide is never the answer.

God has given us a great gift of life. Through this life we have the opportunity to move closer to Him and closer to the Heavenly Abode. However, if we throw away this opportunity, then we lose the chance. People, especially youth, make the tragic mistake of thinking that suicide will give them a "fresh start" on a new life. But it is the exact opposite. By committing suicide they condemn themselves to lifetimes of not only the exact problems they faced in this life, but also to the negative karma accrued by killing themselves. Thus, their next life will inevitably be much more problematic and much more painful than this one.

14.   *Some people donate arms, eyes, and kidneys after death. Some cultures give their bodies to vultures. Do these good deeds at the end of life help the soul for rebirth. Are they beneficial to the soul or does the soul have to suffer for the broken body?*

Whatever we do, in life or death, that helps others is a good deed. We should help others as much as we can during life, and if in death we can help them further, then we should do that as well. There is a tradition when saints die that they are not cremated, but rather their bodies are floated down Ganga. The reason for this is so that the fish and other animals can gain nourishment from their bodies. The lives of saints are lived for humanity, and even in death they want every cell to be useful to another creature.

So, the soul certainly does not have to suffer through donating organs, and – in fact – it is benefited. Our souls progress and benefit through every good deed we perform, whether in life or in death.

FASTING –
ITS MEANING, ITS PURPOSE

Today, fasting has become a great trend across the world. In any bookstore you will find volumes of literature extolling one fast or another. There are juice fasts, water fasts, fruit fasts, etc. Fasting is frequently heralded as the "miracle weight loss" for those who have tried all else without success.

Connection with the Divine.

However, while fasting is certainly of great health benefit, to define it merely as a type of "diet" is to undermine one of the oldest and most sacred spiritual practices. Fasting has been used for millennia by the rishis, saints and sages in order to purify their bodies, minds and souls and to bring every cell of their bodies into connection with the divine.

A True Fast

A true fast, undertaken with understanding and discipline has the power to cure most ailments of the body, mind and spirit. For the body, a fast restores all systems of the body – the nervous, circulatory, digestive, respiratory and reproductive systems are all regenerated. The toxins and impurities in our blood and tissues are eliminated and our system becomes rejuvenated. It is a rare man who dies from under-eating; however, the majority of all today's terminal illnesses are rooted in over-consumption.

A fast also is one of the best ways of controlling our mind and senses. Fasts have been used for millennia to subdue passion, anger and lust. They allow us to withdraw our senses from the outside world and become refocused on our own divine nature and our connection to God. Additionally, during this period of sadhana, of austerity, of restraint one realizes that one is truly the master of one's body, not vice versa.

Unfortunately today, even the Indian community seems to have forgotten much of the purpose of a fast. Today, you will see people with plates overflowing with puris and pakoras who say they are fasting. There are phalharI chapatis, saboodana kichari and so many other hearty foods that we barely even notice it is a fast. I have heard that there is even a recipe for phalharI pizza dough!

On the one hand, it is wonderful to see such a proliferation of the idea of phalhar, and I am glad to see that observing weekly fasts, or fasts on Ekadashi are rituals which have not been lost as we enter the 21st century.

However, it is crucial to pause and reflect on what we are calling a "fast," for, although the idea of fast is still upheld with great fervor, its true meaning and purpose is quickly being obscured by the latest phalhar recipes.

Upvas
In Sanskrit, the word for fast is Upvas. This literally means, "sitting near to..." Sitting near to whom? Near to God.

Fasting is a time in which our bodies are light, a time in which our vital energy is not being dissipated through the process of consumption and digestion, a time in which we are free from the heaviness and lethargy resulting from overindulgence.

However, a fast is not meant to be merely a refrain from eating. It is not as simple as just reducing one's caloric intake or avoiding certain foods. Upvas is not a time in which only our stomach is free from excessive external stimulation. It is not a time of mere restraint of the tongue. Rather, it should be a time in which all of our organs are restrained. It should be a time in which all of our organs are purified, a time in which every sense is turned toward the divine.

Our tongues should refrain from both indulgence in food and drink, as well as from indulgence in speech. A fast should also be a time of silence, for we lose much of our vital energy in speech, and through speech our focus becomes diverted outward.

A Fast For the Senses

We tend to think that we only "eat" through our mouths, that our meals are the only "food" our bodies get. However, what we hear, what we see, what we touch – all these things are taken into our bodies as food. Just as pure, wholesome food brings us health of the body, so do pure, wholesome sights, sounds and other stimuli bring us health of the mind, heart and soul. Therefore, when we undertake a fast, we must be equally as aware of purifying the food that we take in through our eyes, ears and hands as we are of the food that we take in through our mouths.

Our ears should refrain from hearing anything other than

chanting of the Lord's name or the quiet of our own thoughts. During a fast we should not listen to rock music, watch TV, or be part of idle gossip. So frequently we see Indians at temple who have spent the whole day "fasting" and then they come to temple and huddle together for three hours gossiping and chatting. Their bodies may be hungry, but their soul has not fasted.

Additionally, that which we see – frequently without even noticing it – penetrates our minds and hearts and changes our perspective. The simple sight of a woman's bare leg may arouse lust in an otherwise simple and pious man; the sight of blood might cause nausea and panic in one who is usually calm; the sight of a enemy might immediately evoke animosity in one who is usually peaceful and loving.

When we fast we must limit all stimuli which we perceive. That is why we should "sit near to God." Sit at the temple – either the temple in your home or in the actual mandir. Or, if you prefer, be with nature. But, make sure that the sights and the sounds which you "imbibe" during your fast are pure, pious, loving and filled with divinity.

During a fast we should also try to quiet our mind as much as possible. So much of our energy is drained each day in our ceaseless, incessant thought process. And where do most of our thoughts lead? Either nowhere or to our own frustration. Rarely do we actually solve anything or find peace through our own pondering. Usually it leads only to more confusion and more questions. Therefore, as we give our bodies a rest from digesting food in our stomachs, as we give our ears a rest from digesting impure thoughts, and as we give our eyes a rest from digesting over-stimulating or sensual sights, let us also give our minds a rest from having to digest our thousands upon thousands of thoughts each day.

Weekly Fasts

Many people fast on a particular day of the week. You will notice, for example, on Monday that many people will say "this is my fast."

The days of the Indian week are in honor of a particular deity or aspect of the divine. Monday, Somvar, is the day dedicated to Lord Shiva. Tuesday, Mangalvar, is the day dedicated to Hanumanji. Thursday, Guruwar, is the day dedicated to the Guru. It is said that on these particular days, that aspect of the divine is in the nearest reach of the devotee. So, for example, devotees of Lord Shiva will observe a fast on Mondays in order to offer their respects to the Lord and to seek his blessings. Seekers who are strongly devoted to their Guru will observe fast on Thursdays, in order to feel "one" with the Guru and to remember him throughout the course of the day.

However, all too frequently, we tend to see that these fasts have become merely ritual; the spiritual aspect has been lost in many cases. People observe fast because they've done it for years, or because their parents did it, or because they were instructed to do so. It is a rare devotee who truly remembers, throughout the course of the day, that aspect of the divine for whom they are fasting. Again, we see plates of puris, pakoras and ladoos, and days spent just like any other day.

This is not the point of the Indian tradition. Indian culture and Hindu tradition are meant to bring us into close contact with the divine. They are meant to open up the infinite, glorious channel between us and God. These rituals were given to help us step out of the mundane world and re-realize our divine connection. If we fill our stomachs with pakoras and ladoos and fried potatoes, are we really very likely to remember God?

The point of the fast is to be light so we can sit comfortably in meditation. The point is to have our energy turned away from food, away from the mundane world and to the divine. The point of being a little hungry is that it reminds us of why we are fasting.

I heard a beautiful story of a great saint who could cure lepers of their oozing wounds. One day a very sick man came to the saint and she carefully lay her hands over his gaping wounds, as they each instantaneously healed beneath the touch of her divine hands. However, when she sent him away, she had left one wound un-treated. Her devotees questioned her, asking why – since she clearly had the ability to cure all the wounds – why would she leave one bleeding? Her answer was beautifully apt. She said, "because it is that one bleeding wound which will keep him calling out to God."

Our lives are extremely busy and filled with so many small errands, appointments and pleasures that we rarely find the time to remember God. I always say that we tell our loved ones, "Oh, I miss you, I miss you" if they are gone for only a few days. But, do we ever find ourselves, with tears streaming down our faces because we are missing

God? Those who do are very rare and very divine. Typically, we tend to remember God when there is adversity. Our child is in the ICU after a car accident and all of a sudden we are chanting mantras. They find a lump in our wife's breast, and we start going religiously to the temple. We are hoping for a promotion at work and so we perform yagna. This is human nature.

So, when our rishis and saints urged people to fast, part of the reason is to remember God. As we are hungry, we remember "Oh, yes, today I am fasting." And then we remember why. Then we remember God. Even if we can not take the day off work to sit in puja or meditation, the constant feeling of hunger in our bodies will still keep us connected to the reason for the fast, and thereby we will be reminded of God throughout the day.

Of course, the ideal is to remember God all the time. The ideal is that He should be ever with us, ever such an integral part of our minute to minute, moment to moment existence that we never feel separate. But, this is rare for people, especially for those who are living in the West (or in Westernized India) and who are constantly inundated with tasks and jobs and with propaganda telling them that they must buy more, own more and obtain more in order to be happy. Amidst all this, many, understandably, find it difficult to keep God in the center of their lives. That is the beauty of the fast – even unconsciously, you are reminded every moment that "today is a special day. Today I am fasting for Hanumanji [or for Lord Shiva, or for your Guru.]"

If we satiate our hunger with platefuls of phalhar, then in many ways we have defeated the purpose.

Ekadashi

Twice a month we observe Ekadashi. The 11th day of each lunar cycle is observed as a special Ekadashi fast. While there are many Ekadashis during the course of the year, each with a slightly different significance, the one most crucial dietary rule during Ekadashi is not to take any rice.

However, Ekadashi is of an importance far greater than simply the restraint from rice and grains. It symbolizes the control of the mind.

Our Upanishads say that to control the mind is the greatest task and the greatest accomplishment. It says that when the mind is under control, all else – the senses, the body – will follow. "The body is the chariot, the senses are the horses pulling the chariot, and the mind is the driver with the reigns in his hands." So, if the driver is calm, pious and peaceful, he will drive the horses and thereby the chariot toward peace, love and God. But, if the driver is tempestuous and intractable, then the horses jump and buck wildly, leading the chariot to thrash here and there, eventually collapsing upon itself.

Our scriptures say we have 10 sense organs, and the mind is the 11th. Ekadashi stands for the 11th, and since the moon is the karaka (symbol) of the mind, the 11th day of the lunar cycle becomes especially conducive to practices which teach us control of the mind.

Ekadashi is, therefore, a fast for the control of the mind. It is said that if a seeker observes even one Ekadashi with true commitment, faith and devotion and if the seeker keeps his mind entirely focused on God during the course of the Ekadashi, that this seeker will be free from all karmic cycles of birth and death.

So, let us all vow to observe fasts – what exactly you eat or don't eat is not as important as the spirit in which the fast is done. There are people who can comfortably go the entire day with no food or even water. There are others who must take fruits and milk. There are others for whom a glass of juice is sufficient. The little details are not so important (unless you are performing a very specific fast for a very specific occasion or ritual). What is important is that the day of the fast is a day for you to be with God. Be light. Be restrained. Be disciplined. Be focused.

A fast is :	*A fast is not:*
• About God	• About food
• A time of reflection·	• A time of hunger
• For peace of the body, mind and spirit	• For pakoras and puris
• A day of discipline	• A diet
• To purify you·	• To frustrate you

The secrets of the ancient science of yoga were passed down from our rishis, saints and sages who came to these very Himalayas for divine inspiration. Through their meditation, austerities and prayers, a treasure-chest of wisdom was bestowed upon them for the benefit of humanity.

Yoga is not a religion. It does not require you to believe in a certain God or to chant certain mantras. It is an ancient science which leads to health in the body, peace in the mind, joy in the heart and liberation of the soul.

These days people take yoga classes to learn all about the various techniques of hatha yoga, of pranayama, of meditation. But yoga is more than that. Yoga is a way of life, and its teachings should penetrate every aspect of your being – from your actions to your speech to your thoughts.

A hatha yoga session has a beginning and an end. You start at 8:00 for instance, and you finish at 9:00. Your pranayama has a beginning and an end. You start at, say, 6:00 and you finish at 7:00. Even meditation – at least in the beginning – has a fixed starting point and a fixed ending point. You sit in meditation for a certain number of minutes or hours each day.

But, what about the rest of the time? How to live yoga even when you are not doing asanas, pranayama and meditation? How to practice yoga in the grocery store? How to live like a yogi in your family, in your work place, when you are stuck in traffic?

They say yoga is an eight-fold path. Asana is one part; pranayama is another; meditation is still another. Two other aspects of this path are called yama and niyama. These can be loosely translated as righteous living. These are the rules for life. By following these moral, ethical, and spiritual guidelines, one's entire life becomes yoga.

In general, yama is exercising restraint over our lower, baser, animal-like instincts, for instance overcoming greed, lust, anger, and envy, and definitely never acting based on these impulses. Niyama can be seen as the embrace of higher, spiritual, humane values, for instance, being generous and selfless, cultivating piety, devotion, compassion, loyalty and humility.

I am not going to go into the details of yama and niyama as these are complex concepts deserving their own articles and books. However, they can be summed up as "do good and be good; do divine and be divine; have the Lord's name in your heart and on your lips, and do His work with your hands."

These moral and ethical principles affect us whether we believe in them or not. People may say, "But, I'm not Indian" or "I'm not Hindu, so I don't have to follow these ethical laws." However, this is not true. As I mentioned, yoga is not a religion. That means NONE of the eight aspects depends upon one's spiritual belief system. Just as shirshasana is beneficial whether one "believes" in it or not, similarly these moral and ethical laws of the universe affect us whether we believe in them or not.

They are like the law of gravity. One can certainly stand on the top of a 10 story building and say, "I don't believe in gravity so I am going to jump." Perhaps as one falls through the sky, one temporarily thinks one has succeeded in defying this pervasive law. Yet, inevitably, one will hit the ground and one's life breath will be immediately whisked away.

Similarly, people may live lives full of greed, anger, lust, arrogance, and disregard for their fellow humanity for many years, thinking they are immune to these natural laws which affect us all. However, eventually, they, too, will hit the ground and be destroyed.

I remember once, when I was abroad, I saw a sign that said, "Follow the rules and enjoy your stay." It is like that in life as well.

There are so many things we do, that perhaps we realize are not right, but we do them anyway. We lie, we covet things which are not ours "Oh how I wish that beautiful car were mine instead of his," we harbor bad thoughts about each other, "Oh if only he would fall sick, then I could have his job." We deny these to ourselves or we rationalize them with excuses. However, if we are going live truly yogic lives then we must subject every area of our life to scrutiny.

For example, what we eat...is our diet in concert with a yogic life? I know that people are learning a lot about satvic food, which means food that is fresh, easily digestible and leads to health of the body and peace of the mind. However, I am not going to talk about the intricacies of a satvic diet. Rather, I simply going to ask, "are you vegetarian? Do you teach vegetarianism to your children?" There is virtually nothing we can do our bodies that is more contrary to the yogic life than eat meat.

How can we be true yogis, full of life, if our bodies are graveyards for dead animals? How can we be at peace if our food choices bring pain and suffering to others?

Additionally, one of the most important aspects of "yoga for daily life" is honesty. How many of us consider ourselves honest people? How many of us can say that we do not tell lies? We would very much like to believe that we are righteous, honest people and that we are passing these values onto our children. Well, if we eat meat, we can not say that we do not tell lies. Here is why: if we wanted to be honest and still eat meat, we would have to go outside, chase down a live cow, and bite right into it. Or we would have to go to one of those chicken "farms," take the animal while it was still alive, tear its head off, pull out its feathers and eat it raw.

Of course, we do not do that. Instead, we order a hamburger. We can not even call it what it is, let alone kill it ourselves. So, we call it beef, instead of cow. We call it pork instead of pig. We call it poultry instead of chicken. And we eat it packaged in neat, nice ways that allow us to forget what we are eating. How many people stop and think that the thing between the tomato and the bread on a hamburger used to be a living, breathing creature? That it was someone's child? We can't. We can not even admit to ourselves what we are doing. How then, can we consider ourselves honest people if we are lying every time we eat? And these are not lies that only cause misunderstanding; these are not "little white lies." These are lies that are killing our planet, our animals and ourselves.

This is what the true yogic life is —contemplation, introspection. We ask ourselves, "what right do I have to take the life of another?" We must pause and think about the decisions we make.

Additionally, a yogi is calm; a yogi is centered; a yogi is in peace, not in pieces. We can not be calm and in peace if we eat meat. Bloody food leads to bloody thoughts. Eating an animal with stress hormones coursing through it, leads to stress in us. Let me explain: When animals (humans included) are threatened, we secrete large amounts of hormones. These numerous hormones are frequently referred to as adrenaline. Their purpose is to prepare our body to fight, to save our lives. Have you ever noticed that when you get scared, a lot of things happen inside you? Your heart beats fast, your digestion stops, your palms sweat and your physical impulses become very good and sharp. These are the result of the hormones. And they prepare us to either fight or run away. Thus, they are sometimes called the "fight or flight" hormones.

When an animal is about to be killed, its body is flooded with these stress hormones which remain in the animals' tissues. So, when we eat those tissues, we are ingesting those hormones (which are the same as our own bodies make). Thus, our own bodies become flooded with these "fight or flight" chemicals, making us even more prone to simple survival instincts.

Thus, the saying, "you are what you eat," comes alive. If we eat stress hormones, then we are eating terror and of course it is no wonder that we can not find peace in our lives.

So, if you are a vegetarian, great. It will not only improve your health, but it will change the very nature of your being. If you are not a vegetarian, then at least think about it. The yogic life is one of contemplation, honesty and integrity.

Additionally, how our food is prepared is as integral to our overall health and peace as what we eat. I am not going to go into all the details here, as there is not space, but it is very important our food is prepared with love, with devotion and with purity. The energy of preparation is absorbed into the food, and — just as the animal's stress hormones affect our own bloodstream — we are physiologically affected by the energy of the cook and the place of preparation. Thus, chant, sing, meditate while you cook and encourage devotion in those who cook for you. Eat pure, fresh food. Then, you will see the magic of it!

So, if being a vegetarian and taking care of the food you eat is all you can do right now, then do it. But, let me go further and explain how to let "yoga" saturate every aspect of your life. For, remember there is both yama and niyama.

Yoga is not simply yama, or refraining from lower instincts. It is also niyama, the embrace of and adherence to higher principles and laws. Remember what we said about, "follow the rules and enjoy your stay."

But, how to put these laws into daily practice? How to truly live and breath yoga instead of simply following a set of rules like a robot? Let me give you three capsules – a multivitamin – you can take every day. If you take all three every day, and let them deeply saturate your being, then you will experience true health of body, mind and spirit. Then, you can say you are truly practicing yoga.

A) MEDITATION : I always say that meditation is the best medication for all agitations. People have so many troubles today, mainly related to the stress in their lives. To address this anxiety, this sleeplessness, this inability to simply be content, they may take pills or fill their lives with excessive material "pleasures". For example, when people feel stressed they may attempt to forget about it by going to the movies, or by getting drunk or by indulging in simple sensual pleasures. Yet, these are not solutions. They do not address the underlying issues. They are simply band-aids to a wound that runs deep beneath the surface.

Yet, meditation will truly calm the mind, fill the heart with joy and bring peace to the soul. And the serenity and joy lasts throughout the day and throughout your life. Meditation is not like a simple diversion which works only as long as you are actively engaged in it. Meditation is not like a pill which quickly wears off and carries unpleasant side-effects. Rather, meditation brings you into contact with God; it changes the very nature of your being. It brings you — immediately — back to the world from which you truly come: the realm of the divine.

As you sit in meditation you will realize the insignificance of that which causes anxiety; you will realize the transient nature of all your troubles. You will realize the infinite joy and boundless peace that comes from God.

You will learn (or perhaps you have already learned) meditation techniques. Do not worry if you can't do it perfectly, or if it is difficult, or if you can't remember everything the teacher said. The point is to do it. Make a time that is "meditation time." It's okay if it's only 5 minutes or 3 minutes. Don't worry. Just do it. Do not say, "Well, I don't have an hour to sit so I won't bother." Commit 5 minutes to meditation each morning. Then you will see the magic of it.

And let this meditation become your life. Do not restrict it to one time and place. Yes, of course, one should have a time set aside for meditation, and there should be a quiet, serene place in which to meditate. However, my point is that even when it is not "meditation time" or even if you are away from home, away from your "meditation place" do not think that you can not meditate. Take 5 minutes at work to simply close your eyes, watch your breath, focus on the oneness of us all, connect with the divine. Eventually, the goal is to let your life become meditation.

B) NO REACTION: We must learn to be calmer in our lives. We must learn to remain still and unaffected by all that happens around us. I always say, "Be like the ocean. The waves come and go, but the ocean stays." Even a large rock, thrown from great distance, with great force, will only cause temporary ripples in a small area. Most of the ocean will remain unaffected.

Yet, we are always jumping into the ocean, right into the waves, letting them carry us. This is our choice. We must learn, instead, to be like the ocean, itself, unaffected by these small, transient things.

So many times we act as though we are the waves of the ocean. Up one minute, down the next, changed by every gust of wind, by every passing boat. Yet, we are not these waves. I am using the analogy of the waves of the ocean, but you must realize that the waves I am really talking about are the waves of anger, anxiety, jealousy, greed, and lust that are just as vast, just as strong and just as restless as the waves of the sea.

We are not waves, pulled this way and that by every passing breeze, by the daily changes in the moon. Yet we act like that.

We act as though we are light bulbs and anyone who wants to can simply switch us on or off. Isn't it true? Can't the slightest comment or look or action of another change our mood 180 degrees? Isn't it so frequent that we are in a wonderful mood and a stupid person at the grocery store is rude to us, or someone on the freeway passes in front of our car, or a friend is cold and distant. Any of these things can immediately switch our mood as though it were a light bulb.

So many times I hear people say, "Oh, I was in such a good

mood, but then Robert called and told me what Julie said about me," or "Oh, that phone call just ruined my day." And the same works the other way. We are sad or depressed and we get a nice phone call or letter in the mail or we eat some good cookies. Then we feel better.

How is that? How can one phone call, or one rude comment from a person have so much control over us? Are we so volatile in our emotions that others have more power over our moods than we, ourselves, do?

Aren't we more than this? Aren't we bigger, more divine, deeper than this? Isn't there more to this human existence than the law of action and reaction? We must learn to keep that light switch in our own hands and to give it only to God. Otherwise we are switched on and off, on and off, all day long and the only effect is that the light bulb burns out!

Let us take whatever comes as prasad, as a gift from God. Let us remain calm and steady in the face of both prosperity and misfortune. We must not lose our vital energy in this constant action and reaction to everyone around us.

But how? How to remain unaffected by the waves of life? This is called spiritual practice! I always say that one of the best ways to learn "no reaction" is through silence. When we are anxious, angry, tense or frustrated, we tend to say things which we later regret; we tend to let our words fuel the reaction in our hearts. So, let us learn the power of silence. Silence on the outside will lead to silence on the inside. This is why so many saints and other spiritual people have "silence time;" it's a time of remembering that we are more than our reactions, a time of tuning in to the Divine Insurance Company, a time of charging our inner batteries.

So, let us learn to meet life's waves with silence — that will make "no reaction" much easier to achieve.

Let me tell you a story. There was once a huge elephant crossing a wooden bridge high above a raging river. The bridge was old and rickety and it shook under the weight of the elephant. As the elephant was crossing the bridge he heard a voice, "Son, Son" the voice said. The elephant looked around him, but he was all alone. "Son, son," the voice continued. When the elephant reached the other side of the river, he saw a small ant crawl onto his nose. "Son," the ant cried. "We almost collapsed that bridge, didn't we?" Our weight was so great, so immense that the bridge almost collapsed beneath us, didn't it, son?" Now, of course the elephant knew hat the ant's weight had been completely irrelevant to whether the bridge would have collapsed. And, of course, he knew that the tiny ant was not his mother. However, what good would it have done to engage in a battle of egos with the ant? Instead, the wise, calm elephant simply said, "You are right, mother, our weight almost broke the bridge."

The elephant retained his serenity, retained his peace and joy. And the ant, for what it's worth, was allowed to continue believing in its own greatness. But, how many of us could be like the elephant? Aren't we always trying to prove ourselves to others? Aren't we always ready to shoot down anyone who trespasses on our egos?

We must emulate the grace and divinity of the elephant

who knew that the only harm would come with the fight. So, we must make "no reaction" the sutra, the mantra for our lives. Then, and only then, will we know real peace.

C) INTROSPECTION : So, in the morning we begin with meditation. All day we practice no reaction. And at night? Introspection. At the end of the day, a good businessman always checks his balance sheet: how much has he made, how much has he spent? Similarly, a good teacher reviews her students' test scores: how many passed, how many failed?

By looking at their successes and failures, they assess how well they are doing. Are the businessman's profits greater than his losses? Are most of the teacher's students passing the exams?

In the same way, each night, we must examine the balance sheet of our day: what were our successes, what were our failures. And for all the successes, all our "plus-points" we must give credit to God. For, we have truly done nothing but let Him work through us. All credit goes to Him. He is the one who saves us, who maintains our dignity and our success.

Just imagine if God had put one television screen on our foreheads and everything we thought was broadcast for the whole world to see! All our reactions, all our inner sarcastic comments, all our judgments, all our weaknesses....just imagine. We would never succeed nor would we have many friends! Isn't it true?

So, it is by His grace that the world does not see our thoughts, only He sees our thoughts. For this, we thank Him. We can say, "Thank you, God, for bringing success to this venture," or "Thank you God for letting me truly make a difference in someone's life today," or simply, "Thank you God for all that went well today."

Our failures, we must also give to him. The fault is ours, definitely. Yet, He is so forgiving and so compassionate that He insists we turn these over to Him as well. We must say, "God, please take these minus points. You know that I am weak, you know that I am nothing. See, see all my failures, all my minus points for even just one day. I can not go even one day without accumulating so many minus points. But, still you love me. Still you protect me from having the world see all my minus points. I am so weak, but you protect me." In this way, each night we check our balance sheet, and we pray to God to help us have fewer minus points, to make us stronger, to make us better hands doing his work, to give us more faith, more devotion.

If we practice these three points every day then our lives will become beautiful. Just as a serious daily asana practice can bring the glow of health to our body, a serious daily practice of meditation, no reaction and introspection can bring the glow of peace, joy and divinity to our lives.

ॐ PEACE - INTERNAL AND EXTERNAL

We talk constantly about peace – it is one of the most popular topics of world discussions today. Peace between nations, peace in our societies, peace in our schools, peace in our families, peace within ourselves. Yet, although billions of dollars and millions of hours are spent each year on think tanks, brainstorming sessions and international conferences, this much-desired peace continues to elude us.

How then to attain it? What is the secret to finding this elusive treasure? Let us discuss it. Because without peace – both inner and outer – all else is meaningless. We can spend millions of dollars building posh downtown centers in our cities, but if we are at war with another country, they will bomb that center to ashes in a second. We can spend thousands of dollars building beautiful homes, but if our neighborhood is violent, our windows will be smashed and our new lawns destroyed. We can work hard and successfully at our jobs, but if we come home to turmoil in the house, there is no joy in the success obtained at work that day, for there is no one with whom to share. We can devote ourselves to obtaining high education, top credentials and a beautiful figure. However, if we are miserable inside, no outer achievement will ever pacify us.

So, then, the root to success in life – personal, familial, societal, national and international success – is first and foremost to be in peace. Yet, it seems that each day this peace slips further and further from our hands.

Recently, in Chicago a woman came to see me. She told me that she was stressed and tense. She said that in order to sleep at night she took pills called "Compose." I told her that she did not need to take Compose. "Just calm your pose," I said. "And you will sleep beautifully at night and be peaceful all day." If we are peaceful inside, humble inside, then nothing outside can ruffle us. So, the first message today is, "calm your pose and you will never need to take Compose."

The mantra of today seems to be "I want peace." "I want peace." Every day people tell me this. They all say, "Swamiji. All I want is peace. Tell me how to find it."

The obstacle and the solution are buried in the statement. Listen: I want peace. What do we have? An "I", a "want" and a "peace." If you remove the "I" and the "want", what is left? Peace. You do not have to look for peace, find peace or create peace. All you have to do is remove the I and remove the want and peace stands there, in its full glory, for all the world to imbibe. It is the "I" and the "want" which obscure this treasure from our view.

So, how to remove these? First let's talk about the I. I is one of the greatest obstacles to peace. I is our ego. I is our sense of ownership, doership and pride. This I says, "I want to be in the center." Isn't it true? We always want to be the ones getting the glory, the appreciation, the prestige. Even when we don't do anything, still we want to be appreciated. This is our downfall.

We have everything these days. Everything is set. We have tea sets, TV sets, sofa sets, video sets, but we, ourselves, are upset. Everything is set and we are upset.
Why? Because of this I that tries to keep us in the center of everything.

So, ideally we remove this I, which is dividing us from our own true selves, dividing families and dividing nations. Yet this is very difficult. Living in the world today, it is nearly impossible to completely remove the sense of "me" "mine" and I. So the next best option is to take this I and to change it. How?

When I stands vertically it is an obstacle. It creates borders, barriers and boundaries between ourselves and others. But take this I and turn it sideways, make it horizontal, and it becomes a bridge – between our families, our communities, and our nations. Let this I become a bridge in the service of the world. If we keep standing so straight and tall and proud as the vertical I, then we will always stand alone. If, however, we turn this I sideways, we say, "okay, let me be bridge, let me bridge chasms instead of creating them, let me stand smaller than others instead of always trying to stand tallest, let me put others in the center instead of myself," then we will stand united and peaceful.

We are so proud, this I is so proud. It thinks, "Oh, I am so successful. I am so good." But, the truth is that we only go to work, God works. We can do nothing without His grace. One minute we are at our desks, acting like king of the world. The next minute, one nerve, just one microscopic nerve in our brain fails and we can no longer speak, or write. One small blockage in one tiny, tiny blood vessel and we can not even go to the bathroom by ourselves. We must be fed and taken care of for the rest of our lives.

So, what to be proud of? He works. We just go to work. As soon as we realize this, then we can take our little I and merge it in the big I, the universal I, the divine I. Then, we surrender our lives and our every action to Him. Then we say, "God, let my tiny drop of water merge with Your great ocean. Let me be a tool for Your will and Your work."

It is through this selfless surrender to Him, that the pain of the I is removed and with that all our troubles and unrest disappear.

We must aspire to be like the sun. Look at the sun: it gives and gives and gives. No vacation. Sun sets here and we think, "sun has gone to sleep." But, if you call India they will tell you, "the sun is shining brightly." So, with no rest, no vacation the sun shines, bringing light and life to all.

And it gives with no discrimination. It doesn't say, "I will only shine on Hindus," or "I will only shine on Muslims, or on Christians." No. The sun is for all. Anyone who wants to open their window and go outside will find the sun there, shining and waiting.

And no hesitation. The sun does not wait for you to pay your bills. All day, all year it shines and never a bill. If you don't pay your electric bills for one month, they will turn off your electricity. No light for you. But, not the sun. The sun never sends a bill.

We must be like that – always giving, with no vacation, no discrimination and no hesitation.

That is the way to merge this I into the divine I and to become peaceful and ever blissful.

Then "want." Remember we said "I want peace." "I" and "want" are the barriers to peace. If you remove them then there is nothing left but peace.

So, first we merge this individual, obstructing I with the divine I, the universal I, and in doing so we become free of the pride, ego and tension which block our attainment of peace.

Then, we remove the want. Our wants, our perceived needs, our desires. What obstacles these are to peace. The more we have the more we want. People always think that if they attain something more, whether it's more money, a better job, a degree, a good husband, then they will be happy.

But, it never works like that. Happiness and peace are found not in the acquisition, but rather in the renunciation of our attachment. I always say, "expectation is the mother of frustration and acceptance is the mother of peace."

It is not the having or the not having that is the issue. The issue is the wanting, the yearning and the expecting. These external things never bring any lasting happiness.

The key to life is sacrifice. One of the most common Hindu rituals is a yagna fire. Perhaps you have seen this. People sit around the fire and place offerings into the fire. With each offering, every time we make an oblation to the yagna, we say, "idam namamah." It means, "not for me, but for You. Not for me, but for You."

The purpose of this is to remind ourselves that although we may be performing the ritual for some benefit of our own, perhaps a wedding or the opening of a new business, or just for inner peace, that even though it appears that we are asking for ourselves, we must remember that everything is for God. We must offer our every thought, every action, every breath, at His holy feet.

So, we must give more and want less. Then, we will know true joy and peace.

But, how to become selfless? How to learn to give more? Prayer. Peace comes through prayer. It doesn't matter what name you use for God or what language you pray in. You can pray to Allah in Arabic, or you can pray to Jesus in English, or you can pray to Adonai in Hebrew, or you can pray to Lord Buddha in Japanese, or you can pray to Lord Krishna in Sanskrit. It doesn't matter.

So, the point is, love God. It doesn't matter what name or form you use. It doesn't matter what language you pray in. Just pray. And then you will see the magic.

The fruit of prayer is faith. The fruit of faith is love. The fruit of love is devotion.

The fruit of devotion is service. The fruit of service is peace.

Through this – prayer, faith, love, devotion and service –

we will all, inevitably attain that sought-after state of inner peace. Then, when we are at peace inside, that harmony will radiate out to all those around us, bringing peace to our relations, peace to our communities, peace to our nations and, finally, peace to the world.

Every day people come to me with problems for which they would like guidance. While the details vary from person to person, and situation to situation there are common themes that run through much of what ails us. The deeper questions, the questions beneath the questions are always the same: how can I be happy? How can I find peace? How can I have meaningful relationships with others? There are so many deeply important principles to live by, so many lessons to be learned in this life on Earth. Let me address a few here.

I) Devote your life to God, not glamour

Every day people go out, go to work, earn money and become more and more prosperous. Yet, at the end of the day, when they return home, they are not happy. At night, when they lie in bed to go to sleep, their hearts are not peaceful, their minds are not at ease. There seems to be no correlation between the amount of money we earn, the number of possessions we buy and our sense of inner peace. Yet, if you ask people what they most deeply want out of life, they will say "to be happy." How then can we find this happiness that appears so elusive? What is the true secret to internal peace and everlasting joy?

The secret is God and God alone. In India, in all villages there is a temple. I remember when I was growing up, and it is still mostly true today, that first thing in the morning, everyone would go to temple. Before beginning the day's tasks, everyone went to the temple, did Pranam to God and took three parikramas (means walking in a circle around Bhagwan). The point of this was not merely ritual. Rather, the parikramas signified "God, I am about to go out and perform my worldly tasks, but let me always keep you in the center, let me remember that all work is for you." Then, they would take prasad — from their tongues to their souls God's sweetness would spread — and they would leave.

In the evening, before returning home, once again, everyone went to the temple. "God, if during this day I have forgotten that you are the center of everything, please forgive me. Before I go home to my family, let me once again remember to whom my life is devoted."

This still occurs in almost every village, especially the small ones, every day. People in those small villages have very little in terms of material possessions. Most of them live below the Western standards of poverty. Yet, if you tell them they are poor, they won't believe you, for in their opinion, they are not. This is because they have God at the center of their lives. Their homes may not have TV sets, but they all have small mandirs; the children may not know the words to the latest rock and roll song, but they know the words to Aarti; they may not have computers or fancy history text books, but they know the stories of the Ramayan and the Mahabharat and other holy scriptures; they may not begin their days with newspapers, but they begin with prayer.

If you go to these villages you may see what looks like poverty to you. But, if you look a little closer, you will see that these people have a light shining in their eyes and a glow on their faces and a song in their hearts that money can not buy.

So, what is the meaning of this? It means, acquire possessions if you want to. Earn money if you want to. There is nothing inherently wrong with being prosperous. It's wonderful. But, remember what is truly important in life, and that is God. Only He can put the light in your eyes, the glow on your face and the song in your heart.

II) *Giving is Living*

There is an old adage that says, "it is better to give than to receive." Yet how many of us actually live by this? How many of us would give to another before taking for ourselves? It is not simple sacrifice I am talking about. Sacrifice implies some level of suffering. It implies that one is forsaking something one wants out of duty to another. While there is a great deal of spiritual value in the lessons of sacrifice, this is not what I am talking about. For, in true giving, there is no suffering. One does not forsake anything. The giving itself becomes its own reward. People talk about cycles of life. For me, the true cycle is: giving is living, living is learning, learning is knowing, knowing is growing, growing is giving and giving is living. This is the true cycle of life.

I have heard it said that "All that we have will some day be given away. Let us open our hearts and give with our hands so the joy of giving is ours and not our inheritors'."

This is truly the message to live by. Embedded within this phrase are many important factors. The first is the fact that we can take nothing with us when we leave this Earth. We expend so much time, mental energy and physical energy to acquire material possessions. Yet, we come into this world with nothing and we leave with nothing but the karma accrued from the lives we lived. Hence, we must re-evaluate the drastic measures we take and the stress we go through to acquire more and more. That which marks our life, that which lives on after we have departed is that which we gave while we lived.

The second important message in the above phrase is the idea of the "joy of giving." Giving truly is a joy. We think we will be happy if we get this or get that. But, that happiness is transient. Watch a child with a new toy, for this is a beautiful example of the happiness which is possible through material wealth. The first minute, the child is ecstatic. Nothing else matters in the world; he can barely contain his exuberance. Within a mere few minutes, you can see the child start to get a little bored. She looks around; what else does this toy do? Are there any other parts that came with it? Within a matter of hours the toy is lying behind the couch, and will only be picked up by the child's mother or father in an attempt to either straighten the house or re-stimulate the child's interest.

Yet, then when the child's interest is completely faded, watch the child give this toy to a younger brother or sister. Watch how he/she loves showing what the toy can do, loves telling everyone that "I gave this toy," loves watching the sibling enjoy it.

Isn't this how life is? The pleasure you get out of an old sweater or a dress you wore once or some mechanical appliance that you just "had to have," is minimal. Yet, take those clothes or appliances to a homeless shelter; donate them to someone in need. Then you will know real joy. The joy of having given to someone else. This is a joy that will last, it will stay with you, it will not fade, but rather will inspire you to give even more. So many times we regret having bought something. "Oh, why did I waste my money?" we say. Yet, I have never once heard anyone regret that they gave something to someone in need. I have never heard anyone say, "Oh why didn't I let that child go hungry?" or "Why did I help that charity?"

So, remember, old adages may have a great deal of meaning for today. "It is better to give than to receive" is one of those adages.

III) Leaving is always Losing

So many times in life, when something is not going our way, we attempt to solve the problem by leaving the unsatisfactory situation. Sometimes this works, but usually it doesn't.

The real lesson in life is to live with it, not to leave it. It is by living with situations that seem difficult that we can truly attain peace and non-attachment. It is in these circumstances that we learn that happiness can only come from God, not from one environment or another.

If you are with God, everywhere is Heaven, and you would never want to leave anywhere. You would see every place as an opportunity to learn, to grow or to serve. However, that is not how we typically live our lives. Rather, we say, "Oh this is Hell!" and we leave. Yet, if He is with you, how can you be in Hell? Hell is due to lack of Him. If the spiritual corner in your heart is not there, you will be cornered everywhere. So, the goal of life is to develop that spiritual corner, to be with Him, not to leave where you are.

IV) Be Devoted on the Inside, Perfect on the Outside

Your mind should be always with Him, yet your hands should be doing His work. People think that in order to be spiritual, or to "be with God" one must be sitting in lotus posture in the Himalayas. This is not the only way. In the Gita, Lord Krishna teaches about Karma Yoga, about serving God by doing your duty. It is the duty of a few saints to live in samadhi in the Himalayas. Their vibrations and the global effect of their sadhana is extraordinary. However, this is not what most people's dharma is. We must engage ourselves in active, good service; that is truly the way to be with Him.

In one of our prayers, called Sita Ram, it says, "Mukha men ho Rama-nama, Rama-seva hatha men." This means, "Keep the name of the Lord on your lips and keep the service of the Lord in your hands." Let your inner world be filled with devotion to Him, and let your outer performance be filled with perfect work, perfect service. I once heard a story about a man who spent 40 years meditating so he could walk on water. He thought that if he could walk on water, then he had truly attained spiritual perfection, that he was then truly "one" with God. When I heard this story, I thought, why not spend 40 dollars instead, buy a boat to cross the water and spend the 40 years giving something to the world? That is the real purpose of life.

However, there must be both the devotion and the service. We can not develop one at the expense of the other. We can't be truly perfect on the outside unless we are devoted on the inside, for only then will God's work shine through us in a beautiful and perfect way. Similarly, we can not say we are truly devoted on the inside unless we are doing perfect work on the outside.

These pearls I have given you are only a few. However, like any jewels, if they are pure and precious enough, they are priceless, regardless of the size. If you follow these and let them purify your life, they will bring you more prosperity than all the diamonds in the world.

 OVERCOMING FEAR

A group of visitors just came to Parmarth Niketan from America. They were a beautiful, dedicated group. In our question-answer session, one woman said to me with tears in her eyes, *"How do you overcome fear? I live my life so afraid all the time. The object of my fear changes as time passes, but the fear remains."*

In my opinion, this omnipresent fear is the most insidious obstacle to our peace, happiness and progress in life.

When I say fear, I don't necessarily mean terror. But, rather I mean all that makes us anxious, nervous, tense and in need of controlling our surroundings. The root of fear is distrust. We have been betrayed, injured, abused. We decide that the world and those around us can not be trusted. In this way, we lose that faith which is so crucial.

What is the answer? The answer to fear is to firmly root ourselves in God (by whatever name, whatever form you chose). When we realize that God is always with us, always for us, we will never be afraid regardless of the circumstances.

Sure, our family and friends may betray us. They may injure us. But, if we give ourselves to God, if we make our relationship with Him our first priority then we will never be broken inside; we will always be cared for.

There is a story of a very powerful king. This king prided himself on being generous and caring for all his subjects. He would often boast that no one in his kingdom was hungry or cold or impoverished. Once, a holy man came to see the king. The king told the holy man how he provided for everyone in the kingdom so well. The holy man asked the king to come for a walk. While they walked in the forest, the king picked up a large rock by the side of a stream. "Break the rock," he ordered the king. The king looked surprised but immediately told his servant to smash the rock. As the rock broke open they saw a small frog, living peacefully in the nutrient-rich water which had gathered inside the rock. "Have you provided this as well?" the holy man asked the king. The king realized that he could not possibly provide something as perfect, as intricate as this food and shelter for the frog. He realized that it is really God who provides for all His subjects

We must realize that if God can provide for even the smallest insects, He certainly will provide for us. I heard a beautiful story of a young boy on a ship. The ship was trapped in a large storm and waves rocked the boat furiously. The passengers screamed and cried and held each other for dear life. In the midst of this terror sat a very young boy, calm, composed and angelic. When asked why he did not cry he answered, "My mother is here, so I know everything will be all right." This feeling we must cultivate. If God is here, if God is with us all the time, then everything will always be all right.

We take out millions of dollars (or pounds or rupees...) of

insurance to protect our homes, our property, our cars. But, what about our lives, who will protect our lives? We must remember our Divine Insurance Company. We must place all of our faith in Him. He will never betray us, and we will rest assured knowing that we are in the best of hands.

One time I was on an airplane flying to Chicago. It was winter time and the plane hit a great deal of turbulence and stormy weather. The captain's panicked voice came over the loadspeaker that everyone should assume crash position. The passengers screamed; some even fainted. I was sitting next to a very respected professor. As every thing descended into chaos I was calmly working on my notepad. "What are you doing?" the professor asked me. "How can you work? The plane is going to crash. What are you possibly working on?"

I told him, "Professor, I am working on my speech. See, I know that I will be all right. I have perfect faith in God. So, if we survive, I will have to give a speech on what it was like to survive this crash. And my English is not so good so I must prepare myself in advance. And if, by chance, God decides to bring us all home to Him, then I won't need the speech. But, at least I am prepared."

We must realize that we are God's children. Just as a child is never afraid when the mother is near, so we must never fear. Fear immobilizes us. It freezes us. It prevents us from thinking clearly. And most of all, it serves no purpose. No tragedy has ever been prevented by fear. No catastrophe has ever been averted by anxiety. No, calm, serene, wise understanding of the situation coupled with undying faith is what is needed.

There is a beautiful story of Swami Vivekananda. He was giving a speech in America. His message to the world was, "Stand up. Be fearless. God is with you." To test his faith, some people staged a scene during one of Swamiji's lectures. In the middle of the lecture gun shots rang out and bullets whizzed past Swamiji's head. The audience screamed and ran for cover. Some dropped to the floor to protect themselves. Only Swamiji remained perfectly calm and composed. Later, he explained as follows: "the bullet which is not meant to take my life will never hit me, even if fired from point-blank range. The bullet which is meant to take my life will kill me, even if I am protected by 100 guards."

So, let us renew our faith in the Supreme. Let us give away our fears, our anxieties. Let us put all our insurance in the Divine Insurance Company. Let us realize that everything is just as it is supposed to be. We are in the lap of our Mother. How can anything go wrong?

ॐ PRANA PRATISHTHA CEREMONY:
ITS MEANING

A Hindu Temple is a sacred place, endowed with divine energies and powers. At the heart of each temple lie the deities, to whom we bow and pray in worship. Why is it, though, that these statues, these "idols" are worshipped as God? How did they come to be infused with divine characteristics? The answer is the Prana Pratishtha ceremony.

People say that Hindus are idol worshippers. We are not. We are ideal worshippers. It is not the plaster and marble and stone we revere; rather it is the presence of God which has been transmitted into these otherwise lifeless statues. The rites and rituals of Prana Pratishtha are followed strictly according to the Agamic texts. Prior to installation, priests who have been well trained in vedic rituals, perform specific mantras and pujas which have been shown to endow an inanimate object with divine life and energy.

These mantras and rites begin with the simple man who sculpts the stone. He is not an ordinary artist. Rather, he is one who has been blessed with the ability to create a physical manifestation of God. He performs puja and prayer prior to and during the sculpting. He maintains, in his mind, the vision of the deity he is sculpting. He prays for this God to come to life in his statue. His work area looks more like a temple than an art studio. So, from the very first moment, the stone is treated with reverence and piety, preparing it to carry the force of God.

Then, when the murtis are finished and taken to the temple, the special Prana Pratishtha ceremony typically lasts for five days. During this time, numerous special rites and rituals are performed and mantras are chanted. It is after this complex set of sacred rituals that the murtis become infused with divine power and truly embody the God in whose manifest form they are created. At this point, they are no longer murtis. They are deities. After this, we no longer refer to the stone or other materials of which they are constructed. For, they have become sanctified and are now only a physical manifestation of aspects of the Supreme Godhead. They are no longer marble. They are now divine. "Whatever form of Me any devotee worships with faith, I come alive in that form." (Bhagavad Gita).

Some people may ask why we need deities, if God exists everywhere. It is very difficult for most people to envision the un-manifest, ever-present, all-pervading Supreme Being. It is easier for us to focus our attention and our love on an image of Him. It is easier to display love, affection and devotion to a physical deity than to a transcendent, omni-present existence. Additionally, through the Prana Pratishtha ceremony and through our own faith and piety, this image of Him truly comes alive and become Him. So, by worshipping His image with faith and love, we arrive at His holy feet.

In the Srimad Bhagavatum, Lord Krishna says, "Whenever one develops faith in Me – in My manifest form as the Deity or in any other of my manifestations – one should worship Me in that form. I exist within all created beings as well as separately in both My un-manifest and manifest forms. I am the Supreme Soul of all." (Canto ll, Chapter 27, Verse 48).

ॐ MEIN TO KAB SE TERI SHARAN
MEIN HUN

Mein to kab se teri sharan mein hun.
*Oh Lord, I have been waiting and waiting for you,
for life after life, birth after birth.
When will you come and take care of me?*

Meri or tu bhi to dhyaan de.
*Please, Oh Lord, I am at your holy feet, yearning for
you. Please pay just a little attention to me.*

Mere man mein jo andhakaar hai.
*Oh Lord, my heart and mind are flooded with a
darkness known only to you. You know how weak I am.
You know how plagued I am by the darkness.*

Mere Ishwar mujhe gyaan de.
*Please Oh Lord, ocean of mercy, ocean of compassion,
shine upon me the light which will remove this darkness.
Bestow upon me the light of understanding and wisdom
so I may remain true to you in spite of the trials and
tribulations of life.*

**Chahe dukh ki rehn mile to kya,
chahe such ki bhor khile to kya.**
*Let me be filled with divine bliss and acceptance in every
circumstance. Whether it's the dark night of sorrow or
the dawn of joy.*

Patajhar me bhi jo khila rahe,
main vo phool ban ke rahun sada.
Make me the flower which always blossoms,
whether it's spring, summer, winter or fall.
Even in Autumn, when all others are dropping
let me continue to blossom.

Jo lute na fiki pade kabhi,
mujhe vo madhur muskaan de.
Give me the sweet, loving smile which never fades,
even during times of adversity.

Teri aarati ka banoon dia,
meri hai yahi mano kaamana.
Oh Lord, I have only one desire: make me the lamp of
your aarti. Let me be the flames which burn with
devotion for you, and which are so bright they shine
your divine light on others.

Mere praana tera hi naam lein,
kare man teri hi aaraadhana.
Gunagaan tera hi main karoon,
mujhe vo lagan Bhagawan de.
Let my every breath chant your name.
Let my heart beat only for you.
Let my every action be in your service.
Let not only my lips sing your glories,
but let my heart also sing your glories.

Mujhe mein hai raag aur dwesh bhi,
ninda paraayee mein karoon.
Oh Lord, I am afflicted by attachments and jealousy.
I am burdened by the habit of condemning others.

Aahenkaar ko Prabhu har lo tum.
Oh Lord, please remove me from this darkness.
Annihilate my ego, my arrogance, my anger,
my attachments.

Mujhe divyata ka daan do.
Please bestow upon me the gift of divinity. Make me
pure. Make me divine. Oh Lord, Bless me, Bless me.

Tera roop sab me nihar mein. Tera darsh sab me kiya
karoon. Mujhe vo nazar Bhagwan de.
Give me that divine sight whereby I see only you, only
your beautiful image in all I behold.

PRAYER

Prayer is calling back home.
Prayer is, in essence, coming home,
for it brings us into connection with our deeper selves.
It is the way we speak to God,
and its beauty and poetry and devotion should match
that in our hearts.
Prayer is the broom that sweeps out our hearts,
so the home we offer to God is an immaculate
and pure one.
Prayer is a time when our mouths, our minds and our
hearts are filled with the glory of God,
when we simultaneously speak, think
and feel our love for Him.
Prayer is the blanket that wraps itself around our souls
and keeps us warm and cozy.
Prayer is the water that quenches the thirst
of a man lost in the desert.
It is the stars that glisten in the dark of night,
giving light to all those who may need it.
It is the sun that shines in the middle of winter,
coaxing the flowers to open their petals.
It is medicine to the sick, food to the hungry, and
shelter to the homeless.

1) When and why should one offer prayer? Is there a specific time of day for it?

Prayer should be done anytime and all the time; anywhere and everywhere; for any reason and for all reasons. When we speak to God, that is called prayer. Therefore, prayer should be a minute to minute, moment to moment, integral part of our lives. Prayer makes us God conscious, it brings us into divine connection. It takes our focus away from the material world and into the spiritual world.

There are, of course, days which are seen as particularly auspicious for offering prayers, certain holidays which have special significance. Additionally, there are 3 times each day when it's particularly important to pray. The first is when we get up. We dedicate our day to God, "God, this day is yours. Guide my actions, speak through my voice, make my hands your tools." Then, at the end of the day, we offer the day to God, whatever we have done – good and bad – we lay at His holy feet. Our successes are due only to His grace, and only He can take care of our weaknesses. Also, before each meal, we offer the food to Him, so that it becomes prasad, nourishing our being with not only calories and vitamins but with His divine light.

However, although certain times and certain days are especially important, the goal is to make every day a holy day; start every day with prayer. Fill every day with prayer. End every day with prayer.

2) Should prayer include mantra, japa, puja, archana, yagna or havan? If so, why?

Mantras and japa help us to concentrate. We live in a world that is overflowing with sensory pleasures and stimulation.

Our lives are over-busy with work, errands, chores, etc. Therefore, it is very difficult to simply still the mind. Mantras and japa and special pujas serve as bridges between this world and the divine realm. They offer us a way to transverse the water which may seem impassable.

They say a mantra has 3 essential components: we must simultaneously picture the mantra, hear the mantra and taste the mantra. It is an experience of the entire being. A mantra is not only the experience of the hand or of the tongue. It must fill our beings

Mantras and japa also purify our minds and hearts. After practicing them for awhile, they become automatic. Typically our unconscious thoughts are filled with trivial matters – conversions we have had or expect to have, groceries we must buy, what we will cook for dinner, or even a persistent commercial jingle. However, by practicing mantras and japa, these other thoughts get pushed aside by the automatic power of God's name. Soon, the mantra and japa will become as unconscious and automatic as the other thoughts. It is like if you hear a song on the radio over and over, during your drive to work, that song will play in head all day long. Similarly, if you try to do your mantra or japa as much as possible, it will eventually become automatic. Your mind will no longer be filled with trivial thoughts and worries. Every free moment of thought will be filled with God.

Also, just like a mother can not ignore her child who cries out, "Mom, mom, mom, mom" so will God be always present with His devotees who chant His holy name. However, these things are means to the end of God realization. They are the means, not the end themselves. Once we develop that close, intimate bond with God, mantras and japa become less necessary. Imagine that you love someone wtih all your heart. You don't need to take a mala and recite her/his name over and over again with the beads of the mala in order to remember him/her. Your heart automatically remembers. Similarly, once we have that deep love for God, we don't need to continue doing japa to bring us into contact with Him. We will be in contact all the time. Our lives will become our japa.

3) Should one chant shlokas during prayer? Does the mantra given by a Guru have any significance? If so, why?

There are so many different shlokas and prayers; it is impossible for me to say – in a general sense – which ones we should practice. This is a reason we have the tradition of gurus. After much thought and meditation, the guruji will tell the disciple which mantra to recite. However, until you have a sadguru, you can take any name of God, whatever form attracts you most. All of His names are holy; all of the mantras praising Him bring you to His feet.

Yes, a mantra given by a sadguru has special power, special significance. A guru transmits not only the words of a mantra, but the tradition and the sadhana of so many enlightened ones. He is giving you not only his wisdom but also the wisdom of his saduru and his guru's guru. So, a mantra from a guru carries with it the guru's light and the guru's understanding and the guru's love.

However, I always say that what matters is your faith, your *shraddha*. That is your real mantra. The words themselves are not nearly as significant as the heart that recites them. It reminds me of a story: a young boy went to church with his father. During the service everyone was offering different prayers to the Lord. The little boy heard so many different prayers recited by so many different people. Then it came time for the "silent prayer." The minister said, "everyone now close your eyes and offer your prayer to God." The little boy didn't know any prayers; he was too young. So, as he closed his eyes, he spoke silently to God, "God, I have heard so many different prayers today. I don't know which one to offer you. I don't know which prayer you will like. And, besides, I don't even know any of them by heart. The only thing I know how to recite is the alphabet. But, I know that all the prayers come from these 26 letters. So, let me recite the alphabet to you, and then you can make whichever prayer you like best out of these 26 letters." And the little boy began to recite, "A,B,C,D,E,F,G..." in his head to God.

I want you to know that God is so happy with the simple alphabet from that little boy, who is so filled with love and faith. So, when we recite our complex sanskrit slokas, let us make sure we are doing so out of shraddha and piety rather than out of ritual and habit.

4) Should prayer include namsmarana (remembering the name of God), namlekhana (writing the name of God) or chanting His name on beads?

All of these are useful. They bring us out of glamour consciousness and into God consciousness. They focus our mind on something divine. However, they must be done in the right spirit. It is not enough to spend your days writing God's name in a notebook. His name must be on our lips, in our hearts, and in our thoughts, not only in our notebooks. The ultimate goal, as it says so beautifully in one of our prayers, is to "have His name on our lips and have His work in our hands." That is the goal. If we spend our days writing His name, or if our hands only have malas in them, then what are we doing for the world? Then what is the fruit of this sadhana?

5) Should one recite Gita, Vachanamrut, Hanuman Chalisa regularly each day? If so, how many times per day?

Yes, it is important to recite our scriptures and important prayers like the Hanuman Chalisa and other shlokas. We must recite these as much as possible, so that they become deeply ingrained into our beings. We must recite them so much that we live and breath them, so that they become as much a part of our consciousness as the names of our family, as the job we do at work, as the things that normally fill our minds.

However, the key is not in how many times we recite them, or in how many verses we recite, etc. The key to salvation is in how much we live them. In the Gita, Lord Krishna says, "Bhagwad Gita Kinchidadhita". If we take even one shloka of the Gita, one divine word of Lord Krishna and actually live it in our daily lives, then we will see the true magic!

6) Should one sing hymns in praise of one's deity or tell the story of the Deity's life?

Katha is important for the same reason that reading the scriptures is important. They give us inspiration and understanding and bring us into the lap of God. But, we must remember that Katha is not a social event. Katha is about God's word and God's message. That is why we should attend, not just to see our friends.

7) How much time during the day should one devote to prayer?

We should devote at least 15 minutes in the morning and 15 minutes at night, but as I said, our entire lives should be devoted to God. Ideally, there should not be a distinction between "prayer" time and "work" time; even the work becomes prayer. But, in this world that is difficult, I know. So, at least 15 minutes twice a day.

8) What should one do if one cannot offer prayer at the appointed time while traveling?

We should not ignore our spiritual lives when our bodies are traveling. Our prayers should be offered as soon as we can. Do not worry about the time change or a delay or anything like that. God never sleeps. He is always awake and always for you. You do not have to worry about waking Him up when you reach your travel destination.

9) Can prayer redeem sins?

Yes, definitely. However, prayer should not simply be used as an antidote for sin. We should not think that we can sin as much as we want and then we can just pray it away. That is not how it works. The prayer purifies us so that we no longer commit sins. It makes us pure and holy. In the Gita it says, "Khisipram Bhawati Dharmatma" and "Api Chetsu Duracharo."

10) If a person offers prayers in the morning but does not observe the moral code of conduct during the rest

of the day, will he or she benefit from the morning prayers?

Yes, all prayer is fruitful. But, they will also suffer the consequences of their dishonest behavior. One does not cancel out the other. The real goal of prayer is to make every thought, every action, every word honest and pure and loving. They say that prayer is the broom which sweeps out our hearts. So, when we pray we should ask God to make us more divine, more holy. Then, we won't have to worry about dishonest deeds.

11) What should one bear in mind during prayer?

Prayer has no side effects, no warnings and no precautions. We should offer ourselves fully to the Lord with no fear and no hesitation. That is true surrender. God is all loving, all embracing. It is only our own ignorance that we should fear. God is the shelter from everything harmful. He is the refuge, the salvation.

12) What kinds of prayer bear fruit? What kinds do not?

All prayers are fruitful. No prayers are ignored by God. However, it is not for the fruits that we should pray. The real fruit of prayer is connection to the divine, and that comes with any prayer at any time.

13) What about people who offer prayers out of fear of God?

On the one hand, it is good that they are praying. That is the main thing. However, God should never be feared. He is infinitely forgiving, boundlessly loving and always ready to take us into His arms. It is the temptations of the material world that should be feared. It is those that steer us in the

---

wrong direction and bring us frustration and anguish.

14) Does God heed our prayers? How does one know if God has heard the prayer?

Yes, definitely God listens. But, we must realize there is a distinct difference between hearing our prayers and gratifying our every whim. God listens to everything we say, to everything we think, to everything we feel. However, that does not mean that He will always give us what we ask for. God knows what we need; He knows what is best for us, both in the present and for our future growth. So many times we think we know what we want, think we know what will make us happy. But, only God really knows. Further, what happens in our lives is a product of so many past karmas, in addition to our goals of today.

So, there are many factors in whether or not our prayers are "answered"; but we must never confuse an unanswered prayer with thinking that God has not heard us.

How to know if God has heard us? We must establish a divine connection, a deep and strong relationship with God. We must have antennae in our hearts that are tuned to only one station: God. Then we will know that not only has He heard our prayers, but also that He is speaking back to us. When we speak to God it is prayer. When He speaks back to us it is meditation.

15) Is there any difference between prayer and thoughtful moral action? If so, what is the difference?

Yes, there is a difference, but there should not be. All of our thoughts and all of our observances should be prayer. Typically our thoughts are about relatively mundane things

– our selfish desires, our expectations, our plans. Prayer is typically purer, more devotional. The goal, however, is to have every thought be focused on God, to have every thought be pure and holy.

16) What about when sincere prayer does not bear fruit?

As I mentioned, there are so many factors that are woven together into the fabric of our lives. Our prayers are only one of those factors. Karma plays a crucial role in what befalls us, whether it's success or failure, prosperity or poverty. That is why we must not only *be* good, but we must also *do* good! The more good we do in our lives, the more our prayers will be fruitful.

17) Can prayer which is not supported by action bear fruit?

They say, "God helps those who help themselves." In other words, do as much as you can, and then lay the fruits of your work in God's hands. I always so, "do your best and leave the rest to God."

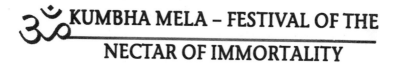

KUMBHA MELA – FESTIVAL OF THE
NECTAR OF IMMORTALITY

Kumbha Mela is one of the most ancient, yet still living, festivals of Indian tradition. The significance of Kumbha Mela dates back far into history; even in the Vedas it is described as a tradition that is already well established. Its occurrence is marked by gatherings of millions at one of four holy places – Haridwar, Allahabad, Nasik and Ujjain the auspicious event occurring at each location once every 12 years.

It is said that even those saints and sages who live in divine isolation, high in the Himalayas, engaged only in meditation and austerities, emerge from the mountains to attend the Kumbha.

The Meaning of "Kumbha Mela"

Kumbha literally means a pitcher. The reference is to the pot filled with the nectar of immortality that emerged after the gods and demons churned the milky ocean. However, the symbolism inherent when we speak of "Kumbha Mela" far transcends the literal translation. A Kumbha Mela indicates the beginning of an auspicious and holy event. A full-Kumbha, occurring every 12 years, also signifies knowledge, happiness and bliss. Our scriptures say :

"कलश्स्य मुखे विष्णुः कण्ठे रुद्र समाश्रितः।
मूले त्वस्य स्थितो ब्रह्मा मध्ये मातृ गणाः स्थिताः॥
कुक्षौ तु सागरा सर्वे सप्त द्वीपा वसुन्धरा।
ऋग्वेदो यजुर्वेदो सामवेदो ह्यथर्वणः॥
अंगैश्च सहिताः सर्वे कलशं तु समाश्रिताः"

The above Sanskrit slokas tell us that the trinity of gods — Brahma (the Creator), Vishnu (the sustainer) and Shiva (the destroyer) — plus all Goddesses, Mother Earth with her seven islands, and all knowledge in the form of Rigveda, Yajur-Veda, Sama-Veda and Atharva-Veda exist in the Kumbha. Thus Kumbha is the symbol of all that is, and all that exists. The Kumbha Mela is a celebration, a festival of the glory of Kumbha.

Astrological and Scientific Background

Indian festivals are not only filled with gaiety and joy, but they invariably have solid scientific and historical foundations, which lead to physical rejuvenation, psychological healing and spiritual upliftment.

It is according to scientific and astrological methods that the place and date of each Kumbha Mela is determined. When the planets, sun and moon line up in a particular way, there is an incredible positive charge in the atmosphere of one of the Kumbha locations. This positive charge affects the water, the air and the entire atmosphere, such that simply being at that special place, and taking a bath in the holy water, is exceptionally conducive to spiritual growth, and to physical and emotional well-being.

The Kumbha Mela is not simply a theoretical ritual, followed blindly. Rather, it is a scientific, historical and thoughtful tradition of the Hindu culture.

Background

The origin of Kumbha Mela lies in the beautiful story of the time when the gods and demons churned the ocean in search of the nectar of immortality.

The fight between good and evil has existed from time immemorial. According to the story, the demons were always fighting with their brothers, the gods. However, the gods did not want to fight; they remained peaceful and calm. This did not deter the demons from killing them, though. Hence, the forces of good were falling to the forces of evil. One day, the devas went to Lord Brahma and said, "We are losing so many of our brothers and sisters in the never-ending war with the demons. If this continues, none of us will be left. Please help us." Lord Brahma told them to go to Lord Vishnu.

Lord Vishnu listened to their story and sympathetically responded, "If you churn the great milky ocean, you will find a gold pot of nectar. The drinker of the nectar will be blessed with the boon of immortality. However, you are not strong enough to churn the ocean yourselves. You must attain the help your brothers, the demons." The gods were in great distress. "But, Lord Vishnu," they said. "If the demons know that the reward of churning will be immortality, they will take the nectar all for themselves. Then we will be in even more trouble. Alternatively, if we hide from them the reason, they will never agree to help us."

Lord Vishnu assuaged them and told them to simply go

and request help from the demons. So, the gods left the abode of Lord Vishnu and successfully convinced their demon brothers to help with the task. The churning of the great milky ocean by the gods and the demons became a momentous event. The rope required for churning was offered by the snake Vasuki, and Lord Vishnu, Himself, became a huge turtle, on whose back they could easily churn.

So, the fantastic churning began with the hope of divine nectar filling the minds of the gods. However, after a great deal of effort, what emerged was not nectar, but poison!! The gods and demons knew that in order to continue churning, they could not simply toss the poison aside. Someone had to drink it. So, a conflict began. Who would drink the poison and thereby allow the historic churning to continue? No one would agree to sacrifice himself, until Lord Shiva came forward and said, "I will drink the poison if it will preserve peace and enable my brothers and sisters to attain the nectar of immortality." The sacrifice Lord Shiva made an example of why He is Maha Deva and all the other gods are simply devas: this selflessness and dedication to the welfare of others.

At last, out of the murky water emerged fourteen precious jewels. At the end, Lord Vishnu, himself, appeared, holding the precious Kumbha in his hands.

However, Indra – the King of the gods – knew that the demons were planning to abscond with the treasure of immortality. So, he immediately signaled to his son, Jayant, who leapt forward, grabbed the pot of nectar and quickly ran away. The demons, however, were stronger and quicker than Jayant and they pursued him relentlessly. Indra sought aid from Jupiter (Guru), Surya (the sun), the moon and Saturn to protect his son and preserve the Kumbha. The long chase lasted twelve days, which was the equivalent of 12 years on Earth. During this chase – which traversed the realms of the Earth, the heavens and the moons — Jayant rested only four times. While he rested, he placed the Kumbha on the ground and a few drops of holy nectar spilled onto the Earth in each place. These four places have now become the four centers of pilgrimage for the Kumbha Mela.

Why and how Kumbha Mela became a National Event

In order to unite the entire nation of India, a festival must appeal to two distinct strata of society: the intellectual, educated class and the average, less educated and more superstitious class. Religious faith is the basis of unity in spiritually inclined people. Spiritual people seek those things which will help them progress further toward the Ultimate goal. Our sages understood this, and thus the mythological stories appeal to the hearts of the masses, and the philosophical message and scientific basis appeal to the educated mind.

Rishis and sages have always shouldered the responsibility of the social, moral and spiritual upliftment of the country; they dealt with problems of invasions, corruption, lethargy and selfishness. The nectar – which manifests in the form of satsang, knowledge, love and grace — is distributed to all, without any discrimination. The great assemblages of sanyasins, yogis, sages and saints reassure and uplift the nation; hence great masses of people rush to the sacred places at the time of Kumbha Mela. Mahatma Gandhi, in his autobiography, writes, "and then Kumbha Mela arrived. It was a great moment for me. I have never tried to seek holiness or divinity as a pilgrim, but seventeen lakhs [17 lakhs equals 1,700,000] of people cannot be hypocrites." Even today, Kumbha Mela requires no advertising. Indian calendars simply note the time and place of the next Kumbha Mela and millions of people flock there with unshakable faith and devotion. It is as if they are responding to a cordial, personal and urgent invitation to attend this function. It is a true miracle of God! One can not even begin to imagine the challenge of organizing such a function and yet it just happens by the grace of the words "Kumbha Mela".

Kumbha Mela in a New Light: The Message for Today

Every nation has its own personality, unique unto itself. Bharat Mata is inherently spiritual by Her nature, and the entire world has long since turned to India for spiritual guidance. However, India has even more to offer the world. Our culture is not only spiritually advanced, but our scriptures have long since taught the messages that are urgent for today's world. For example, India is the only land where rivers, mountains, trees and animals are not only respected, but also worshipped.

In today's age of environmental awareness and ecological conservation, everyone knows that mountains, rivers, and trees are great natural resources which must be preserved, conserved and used wisely. We have seen the devastating consequences of deforestation, over-industrialization and the pollution of our water sources. No one can be blamed for this travesty other than ourselves. Yet, it is Hindu culture that has preached reverence for nature since its inception so many thousands of years ago.

Rivers, especially Ganga, are truly our "mothers." Farming is a primary occupation in India; thus, irrigation is of utmost importance. Ganga and other rivers irrigate not only our farms but also our hearts, minds and souls. It is to our sacred rivers that pilgrims flock for the Kumbha Mela; yet we must remember that these rivers and mountains are sacred and treat them as such. The message of the Kumbha Mela of present times must include a renewed care for the land we call "Mother."

The nectar that Kumbha Mela must disseminate today is a renewed respect for our Earth and her animals, a re-dedication to the laws of our scriptures, and a re-kindled fire of spiritual yearning in our souls. This year, as we celebrate Kumbha Mela just as our ancestors did, we should remember the way in which they lived and the values to which they held. If Kumbha Mela can re-unite us with our sacred roots and with the messages of our scriptures, then it will veritably be giving us the "nectar of immortality." Then, and only then, will we attain true peace and liberation.

ॐ WORSHIP OF THE MOTHER

One of the most important aspects of Hinduism is reverence for the Divine Feminine, the Shakti, in all her myriad manifestations. However, although there are truly infinite ways to thank and worship the Mother, I feel that three ways are most important.

If we hold three of Her aspects close to our hearts, cherish them deeply and thank God for them every day, we can honestly say that we are worshipping the Goddess.

These three aspects are: your mother, your mother-land, and your mother-tongue.

Your Mother

A mother is truly divine. It is from her womb we have come. Our life is a gift from her own; our nourishment flowed from her body. The love that sustains us, that embraces our soul, ceaselessly streams from her heart.

When I say your "mother" I mean many things. Of course I mean the actual mother who gave you birth. But, I also mean the divine Mother of all — the Goddess. In this Mother, we find not only our own mothers, but mothers everywhere. We find Mother Nature, Mother Earth, Mother Ganga.

These Mothers must be seen as divine. For your own

mother, this means treating her with respect, with love, with patience. I know that when we are young, we tend to take our parents for granted, or to become frustrated at their attempts to teach us. We must not do this. We must find, in our hearts, her own blood and her own life. For that is how connected we are.

For Mother Nature and Mother Earth this love and respect means protection. She has given us all that we need to sustain our lives. And we are simultaneously destroying Her. Let us treat our Earth as a Mother. If our own mother were sick, we would not let her simply suffer, decay and die. We would fight tenaciously to bring her back to her full state of glory. Let us give the same to the real Mother. We must not pollute her or waste her. We must nurse her back to health.

Mother Land

Be Western (if you live in the West) when it comes to professional excellence, but be Indian in your domestic life, in your heart. The West has a great deal to teach in terms of external perfection — especially in professional, business and engineering arenas. But, we must not lose our souls in this attainment of external success. Our bodies and our brains may be in the West. But, our spirit must stay with our Mother land.

How to do this? First, have a "happy hour" in the evenings. But make it an Indian "happy hour." Make it an hour whose happiness lasts even when the 60 minutes are up, a happiness without a hangover, a happiness that runs to your soul, not just your bloodstream. The real happy hour is puja, Aarti, being with the family. You spend so many hours each day being Westernly perfect. Spend at least one hour being Indianly devoted. Then, you will see the real magic.

Maha Laxmi is the Goddess of Wealth. We pray to Her for prosperity. Yet, our real wealth lies in our heritage, in our roots, in the ancient wisdom of our scriptures. Let us not forsake the everlasting richness of our culture in favor of transient material possessions. Before we pray for more wealth, let us treasure the wealth we have already been given. This is the real prosperity.

Your Mother-Tongue

This is the language of your soul. Your brain may think in English; your mouth may speak English. But your soul speaks Hindi, or Gujarati or Punjabi or Tamil or Kannad or Sindhi...Do not cut yourself off from the words of your ancestors, for much of the wisdom and clarity is lost in translation.

A dog does not have to learn how to bark; a cat does not have to learn how to meow. A cow does not forsake her own natural "moo" for the chirping of the birds. It is wonderful that you are all learning English and French and Spanish and German. These languages will be of a great help to you in your academic and professional lives. But, your mother-tongue is the thread that connects you to your roots, to your family, to your true essence. Do not sever this connection, for it is the tube through which your life-blood flows. How can you truly know a culture, be part of a heritage, if you can not speak its language?

ॐ UNITED WE STAND, SURVIVE AND FLOURISH

Hinduism is, at its very core, a religion of unity, a religion of inclusion. Our scriptures teach "Vasudhaiva Kutumbakam." The Upanishads say, " Ekam sat viprah bahudha vadanti...The truth is one, but the paths are many." The scriptures explain the differences between the various paths, but never hold one in higher esteem than another. Thus, there is no place in our culture, tradition, faith or religion for exclusion, for prejudice, or for an "us versus them" mentality. One of the great pillars of Sanatan Dharma, and that which has helped it to withstand the test of time, is its unity in diversity, its ability to embrace innumerable sects into its arms.

Unfortunately, today we are seeing these very basic principles uprooted and undermined. It is not only other religions and faiths against which our people seem to be discriminating, but this discrimination is even taking place against members of our own Sanatan Dharma! Today, as I travel the world, I hear people make comments like "Oh, we are not part of *that* katha. That is being done by the *other* temple." Or, "*Our* Janmashtami program is held *here*, and *their* program is held over *there*." Or, "I won't go listen to *that* saint speak. He is not from *our* sampradaya." I hear complaints and criticisms from one group about the others. Suddenly the foundation of our great tradition seems to be splitting and splintering abroad.

This is a great tragedy.

God is one – ultimate, omniscient and omnipotent. He manifests at various times throughout the history of the world when darkness is overpowering light, when evil is vanquishing righteousness, when adharma wields its insidious hand over dharma. Depending upon the time and the need of the people, God incarnates in such a form that it will be most beneficial to those whom He will teach.

The same is true in personal worship – God appears to each of us in the form which is most suited to our own, personal spiritual development. Bhagwan Shri Krishna says "Ye yatha maam prapadhyante," meaning, *"whichever form the devotee worships, in that form I appear."* This does make that particular form inherently or objectively "better" than the others. It just means that is the form which will be easiest for US to relate to and worship.

Additionally, as we talk about the various paths to God — including *Gyan, Bhakti* and *Karma* — which manifest in today's world as various branches of teaching, none is objectively superior to the other. Certain people are more inclined toward scriptural study and philosophy. Others are more inclined toward selfless service and humanitarian work. Still others are more inclined toward blissful love of God and the devotional aspects. For each of these paths, there are numerous branches, sects, and schools of teaching. In this way, everyone, whether they live in India or abroad, can find a particular group with whom to relate, a particular temple in which to worship, and particular practices which appeal most to their own, inherent sensibilities.

However, it must be remembered that this flexibility of Sanatan Dharma is there so that the maximum number of people can achieve the ultimate goal of God realization. It is NOT there so that we can break ourselves off into isolated groups, shunning others and disseminating only the teachings of our particular branch!

Hinduism is a great tree of life. We each live on a particular branch and eat the leaves of that branch for our nourishment. But, we must not cultivate the belief that our branch is superior in any way to the others. Nor must we mistake our branch for the tree itself. No branch is the tree. Only the tree is the tree. Yet, all branches are intricately connected to this tree and depend upon it for their very survival. An isolated branch, split off from the Mother Tree, will quickly become desiccated and perish. It is only by remaining closely connected to the Tree that any branch can survive.

Therefore, let us all choose our personal method of worship. Fine. Let us have our personal *ishta devta*. Wonderful. But, let us not forget that it is the Tree which sustains us, not the branch. That tree is Sanatan Dharma. That tree is our Indian Culture. Every branch stems from the same great trunk. Our roots are the same. It is the same soil which nourishes us. Thus, let us remember that we are NOT separate. Rather, we are one.

The Hindu groups must function like fingers on a hand. Sure one is longer, one is shorter. One is closer to the left, one is closer to the right. One is narrower, one is wider. But, they are part and parcel of the same hand. Only by working together, as a united hand can any beneficial work be done. A finger, by itself is virtually powerless. One, isolated finger, can not do anything to benefit itself, nor anything which benefits the hand, nor anything which benefits anything! It is only by working in conjunction with the other fingers and with the rest of the hand that the fingers' potential is realized.

Similarly, all the Hindu groups are individual fingers – separated slightly, different in outward appearance. At times, they may stay apart. But, when necessary they must come together. They are part of one divine Hand and they must work together for the benefit of themselves, for the benefit of Hinduism and for the benefit of the World.

THE SIGNIFICANCE OF TEMPLES

A temple is not a building. It is the abode of the Lord.
A temple's strength is not in its bricks.
Its fortitude comes from the dedication of its members.
A temple is not held together by plaster and mud.
Its glue is the piety and devotion of the community.
A temple is not simply a place we visit.
It should be the axis around which our lives revolve.

People may ask, "but if God is everywhere, if every living being is a manifestation of Brahma, then why do we need to go to temple?" There are many reasons. The most important reason is that a temple is not only the home of God, but is a concentration of divine energy.

During the installation of the deities (Prana Pratishtha ceremony), the murtis become powerful manifestations of God. The priests chant special vedic mantras and perform special sacred rituals which endow these deities with divine attributes and powers. Therefore, praying before a deity in a temple may give us a greater sense of being in the presence of God, than praying in our own homes.

Additionally, the temple building itself is constructed in such a way as to maximize the concentration of positive, sacred and peaceful energies. The actual structure of a temple is said to represent the resting body of the Lord. The sanctum tower (vimanam) represents His head, the door of the sanctum is is His mouth, the entrance tower (raga gopurum) is His holy foot, and other parts represent His limbs. And, most importantly, deep inside the main structure is the sanctum sanctorum (garbha graha), which is the Heart of the Lord, and it is there that we place the deities.

Ancient rishis and saints could realize God through their meditations. They lived high in the Himalayas or in secluded forests. There were few distractions, and their lives were focused on one thing: attaining the divine vision. They, therefore, did not need temples. Their world was their temple. However, today, our lives are flooded with material desires, with mundane tasks, with logistic concerns. We must get up each day and go to earn a living to feed our families. We must live in a world that indoctrinates us to crave only sensual pleasures and material wealth. It is very difficult for this world to seem like a temple. Therefore, we must have a place which is sacred, a place which is holy, a place in which our sole purpose is becoming one with God, a place in which we hang up our daily concerns and troubles like coats at the door. We must have a place which focuses our mind on the true meaning in life. The temple serves this purpose.

A university student may claim he does not need to go to the library to do his homework – his dorm room is a fine place to study. Theoretically, that is true. The books are the same, the material to be learned is the same. However, we know that in a dorm room he will be constantly tempted by ringing phones, by knocks at the door, by loud music, by the desire to gossip with his friends in the hallway.

However, the library is silent. It is a place devoted to academic studies. There, he will not be distracted. In the library, everywhere he looks he will see other students deep in their work. This environment will provide him not only with quiet in which to study, but also with inspiration from others who are there for the same purpose.

Similarly we go to temple for the sacred environment, for the holy energy in the building itself, for the divine presence of the deities, as well as for the inspiration of others who are focused on God.

However, a temple should not only be a place in which we worship. It should become the focal point of our lives. In the West, many of you have left your extended families back in India. Most of you do not have the luxury of living in a tightly-knit Indian community. Therefore, the temple should become that extended family; it should be your tightly knit community. Your temple should be the place where children come to learn about their heritage as well as to play with their Indian peers. Your temple should be your place of celebration during times of joy, as well as your place of comfort and solace during times of grief. Your temple should feed every aspect of your being: your hearts, your minds, your stomachs and your souls. Then, it will truly be a "mandir" and not only a building.

ॐ THE BHAGAVAD GITA :
QUESTIONS AND ANSWERS

1) What is your favorite holy scripture?

There is a true galaxy of holy scriptures, each one its own solar system of stars and suns. Each contains an unparalleled wealth of wisdom and inspiration from our Rishis. These scriptures are the lamps that shine brightly on the path of righteousness and truth, guiding our way in the dark of night.

However, if I had to choose one, I would say it is the Shrimad Bhagavad Gita. As Pujya Paramhansa Yoganandaji said, "The Bhagavad Gita is the most beloved scripture of India, a scripture of scriptures. It is the Hindu's Holy Testament, the one book that all masters depend upon as a supreme source of scriptural authority." The Gita provides wisdom and upliftment, comfort and solace to people of all ages, from all walks of all life, from all corners of the Earth.

"Bhagavad Gita" literally means Song of the Spirit, Song of the Soul, Song of God. Like any truly divine song, the language of the original lyrics and the religion of the original singer are irrelevant. For once it has been written and sung, the song itself becomes alive, bursting forth across oceans and mountain ranges, breaking all barriers of caste, creed, nationality. Such is the power of a divine song. However, as the original "singer" of the Gita is Lord Krishna, Himself, this is the holiest and most sacred of all the songs of God. Therefore, its power to transform, to heal, to uplift is as limitless as the Singer.

It has been said that the Upanishads are the cows, Lord Krishna is the cowherd, Arjuna is the calf, and the Gita is the milk. But, it is notjust any milk. This milk is nectar that flowed from the Gods with the power to heal the sick, comfort the lonely, guide the lost, uplift the fallen and bring peace to the troubled. The milk is gentle and pure enough for a baby, but strong enough for a warrior.

2) *How and when were you introduced to this holy scripture?*

I was introduced to this incredible work by my Spiritual Master, when I was 8 years old. The Gita was his favorite text and he used to carry it everywhere with him. He said it was the most important piece of wisdom for everyone, regardless of education, caste, or spiritual aspirations. When he initiated me, he gave me my own copy — a small, simple version in the original Sanskrit. I learned Sanskrit through the Gita, through memorizing its entirety. In that way, Lord Krishna's message and His language came alive for me simultaneously.

3) *How much time do you devote each day to the Gita?*

Now, approximately an hour each day. But at the beginning, in my early years, it was my life. Every minute of my day was spent in either meditation, japa, or contemplation on God and the Gita. While I may only spend an hour each day studying the Bhagavad Gita, I spend all 24 hours living the Gita.

4) *What is the impact on your life of the Bhagavad Gita?*

The Gita has made me अस्त (*ast*), व्यस्त (*vyast*), मस्त (*mast*) and स्वस्थ (swasth). What do I mean? First, I became *ast*, emerged in God. I was like the sugar that — when mixed in water — loses itself and becomes one with the water. The sugar was so solid and separate when it sat on the spoon. But, in the vastness of the water, the structure of the sugar simply dissolves.

The Gita became the blanket that wrapped itself around me in the cold and dark of night. I was alone in the forest, and became completely immersed in Lord Krishna; His words spoke to me through the Gita, through my mantra, and through His own voice. They comforted me, taught me, and guided me.

Then, as I studied the message and the wisdom of the Gita more, I learned how to be *vyast*. *Vyast* — in essence — means "doing is being, and being is doing." This is Lord Krishna's message. So many people today assume that a spiritual path is one of idleness, one of silent contemplation high on a mountain top. But, Lord Krishna teaches otherwise. We should be the hands that do God's work — this is Karma Yoga. We should not only be divine, but we should DO divine. "Serve, serve, serve, do your duty on Earth." But, again, *vyast* is a different kind of "doing" than most people do. It is "being" while "doing." What does this mean? It means having your work be prayer, be meditation. All the time your hands are doing, your mind should be being. Have His name be on your lips and in your heart, and have His work be on your hands.

From *ast* and *vyast*, I have become *mast* — ever happy, ever joyful, ever blissful. When you are immersed in Him and His work is flowing through you, what else can you be?

When you are *ast*, *vyast*, and *mast*, you automatically are *swastha* — or completely healthy, and in perfect balance. But *swastha* does not imply only perfect physical health; rather, it is a full health of body, mind, soul and spirit. Every pain, every ache, every discomfort becomes prasad as you lay it in His lap. His love and His presence dissolve all that hurts both within and without. Your body and your soul becomein perfect harmony.

5) *How do you convey the message of the Gita to your devotees?*

The Bhagavad Gita is not abstruse. It is intricate and deep, but neither complicated nor difficult. Its messages are clear. Through the story of Arjuna and the battle, Lord Krishna gives us lessons for our lives. The real Kurukshetra is within us. Each of us is Arjuna, struggling with right and wrong, temptation, fear and frustration. Our bodies are our chariots, being driven all too frequently by our senses as the horses. The mind, ego, desires, lust and greed are the evil Kaurvas with whom we must do righteous battle, from whom we must not shy away in fear and trepidation. If, instead of letting our chariots be driven by our senses, we give the reins to Lord Krishna, we will surely be victorious.

Additionally, the central message of the Gita is to perform your duties diligently and piously, but without any expectation for what the result will be. You must till the soil, plant the seeds, water and tend the seedling, and take care of the tree without any thought of how much fruit this tree will bear. You must be God's gardener, carefully tending the garden but never becoming attached to what will blossom, what will flower, what will give fruit or what will wither and die. Expectation is the mother of frustration, but acceptance is the mother of peace and joy.

Lord Krishna says, "Stand up! Do divine! Be divine! Don't expect, but accept!" Life is about the journey, not about the destination. If the reins of your life-chariot are in His hands, you will be ever happy, ever peaceful. This is the lesson of ultimate surrender that I convey to my devotees. Put all your assets in the Divine Insurance Company, and you will always be taken care of .

6) *How relevant is this message for today's life?*

The message of the Gita is as relevant for people living in the West today as it was for the people of India more than 5000 years ago. It is as relevant for Hindus as for people of all other religions. It teaches Hindus how to be better Hindus, but it also teaches Muslims to be better Muslims, Christians to be better Christians, and Jews to be better Jews. For, if something is really "truth," it must be universal. Truth is not limited to a religious framework. If it is truth, it must pertain to all. Such is the profound truth of Lord Krishna's words.

Like Mother Ganga, like the rays of the sun, the Bhagavad Gita does not discriminate. Mother Gangaji does not bring water to only Hindus' farms. The sun does not shine only on Hindus' flowers. Similarly, the Gita does not provide light and inspiration to only Hindus' minds and souls.

7) *Is the Bhagavad Gita useful for people in the West?*

Definitely. Aldous Huxley said, "The Gita is one of the clearest and most comprehensive summaries of the perennial Philosophy ever to have been made. Hence its enduring value, not only for Indians, but for all mankind."

Perhaps people in the West actually need this wisdom even more. People in the West seem to hold even more tenaciously to their agendas, their expectations, their desires. The message in much of the West is "if you work hard, you will succeed, you will become prosperous." So, people don't work for the sake of being God's hands. They work to reap the benefits, and when the benefits don't come or don't come quickly enough, they are frustrated.

Hence, it seems people in the West need both the message and the comfort of the Gita a great deal. Mahatma Gandhiji said, "When disappointment stares me in the face and all alone I see not one ray of light, I go back to the Bhagavad-Gita...I immediately begin to smile in the midst of overwhelming tragedies and my life has been full of external tragedies. If they have left no visible, no indelible scar on me, I owe it all to the teachings of Bhagavad-Gita." The lives of people today seem colored by indelible scars. I hope they will all turn to the Gita as the remover of pain and the bestower of light. I hope we can all sit together in the lap of the Mother.

8) *All the time you are moving from city to city, from country to country. You are so busy with all of your spiritual and charitable activities. Do you find time to read the scriptures of other religions as well?*
Definitely. I have read the major scriptures of most religions. I feel that the truth is one, although the paths are many. Therefore, each path, each religion has great value for me. I have read Shri Guru Granth Sahib, the holy book of Sikhism, the Koran, and the Bible, as well as numerous other religious works from other religions.

9) *Do you compare these works?*

No. Every book gives an important message, and — in fact — the messages are the same, although the language is different. Each work teaches the message of, "love all, hate none; heal all, hurt none."

If you don't fully understand something (like another religion) you should never criticize it. Instead of criticizing the principles of others, our energies should be spent on following the guiding principles of our own religion. That is what will lead to health and happiness, peace and prosperity.

10) *How can the Bhagavad Gita be useful in achieving salvation and self-realization?*

The Gita provides the guiding principles for both peace in this life as well as for ultimate salvation. When I was in Japan, I saw a sign that said, "Follow the rules, and enjoy your stay." While it is simple and trite, it is also true. The rules for our lives are laid out in the scriptures: do divine, be divine, serve without expectation, love all, surrender to God, etc. When we follow these rules our lives become infused with joy and love and peace. It is when we ignore these commandments or amend them to suit our own agendas that we bring pain and turmoil into our lives. The Gita is a complete yet concise listing of all the teachings necessary to achieve self-realization in this life as well as eternal salvation and liberation.

11) *Does the Bhagavad Gita answer the youth as well?*

Of course. The trials and tribulations of youth are not so different from those of adults: Who am I? What do I believe? What do I want out of life? What is my purpose here? Are these not questions that continue to plague us throughout our lives? Childhood and adolescence are simply times in which the intensity of the questions and the agony caused by not knowing the answers are at their peak. Sure, the logistic concerns of youth differ from the logistic concerns of old age; however, at the core, we are all searching for truth, peace and happiness. The Gita provides this. Additionally, because it was sung by Lord Krishna, himself, the Gita has the miraculous ability to give the reader exactly the answer and meaning he/she was searching for. So, if you open it today in the midst of a crisis at work you will come upon a passage that will speak something different to you than when you open it a year from now, looking for comfort after the death of a parent. Similarly, youth will find a different jewel in the treasure chest than adults will. But, it is still a jewel from the ultimate treasure chest.

12) *In today's changing world, is there something in Gita for all of humanity?*

Definitely. This is what I have been saying. The truth is there for all to see. The sun does not disappear behind a cloud simply because a Christian or a Muslim goes outside. The Bhagavad Gita shows us the way to live with God, to live with each other and to live with Mother Earth in peace and harmony. This wisdom and insight is as changing as the River Ganga, able to address the concerns of each generation, and yet as stable and everlasting as the Himalayas themselves.

ॐ THE YAGNA OF MAHATMA GANDHI

In August, 1998 we celebrated the Golden Jubilee of India's independence, and on January 30, 1998 we observed the 50th anniversary of the assassination of Mahatma Gandhi. The former was an occasion for rejoicing; the latter was an occasion for somber reflection. We won our independence, but we lost a beautiful soul, a true *Maha Atma* (Great Soul). As we revel in the joy of India's freedom, we must not forget the price we paid. Gandhiji was truly the saint of the century, and our Pranam to him should be that we never forget the message of his life.

As we reflect on the greatness of Mahatma Gandhiji's life and the tragedy of his assassination, let us look not only at facts but at meanings. What was the meaning of his life? What was the message of his death? What does he have to teach the world of today?

We can answer these questions with the word "yagna." Yagna was the spirit of his life and the message of his death. Every breath of his life, including the last, was an oblation to his country, his principles and his faith in God. The theme of his life was truly sacrifice.

Sacrifice for his country

Mahatma Gandhi could have been a wealthy attorney. He could have had a life of relative ease and prosperity.

However, he was a man devoted to his country and to Her freedom. Through his tireless effort and his simple piety he led India to independence. However, in spite of national and international acclaim, he never lost his humility, his dedication and his spirit of sacrifice. Rather, the flames of his true yagna to Bharat Mata seemed to only grow until he, himself, was the *poornahuti*, or final offering.

When I was little, a great saint said to me, "देहो देवालयो प्रोक्तः" — A It means that we, as people, always want to be in the center. We always want the focus on ourselves, the recognition for ourselves and the reward for ourselves. We do not actually work or accomplish anything meaningful, but we expend great effort trying to convince all those around us of our inestimable worth. However, Gandhiji was different. He did everything, accomplished everything. Yet he worked and lived with such humility and such piety that he never put himself in the center. This is a great message of his life: "work, serve with every breath, but remain a simple, humble, unattached child of God."

There is a story of a man traveling by train to Porbandar in the same coach as Gandhiji. However, the man did not know that the old man in his coach was Mahatma Gandhi. So, all night long this man lay down on the seat, occupied the entire seat in the coach, pushed Gandhi, put his feet on him, and left Gandhiji with barely enough room to sit upright. However, Gandhi did not fight, or complain. How easy it would have been to proclaim, "I am Mahatma Gandhi. Give me room in the coach." But that is not the spirit of yagna.

As the train pulled into Porbandar the man mentioned that

he was going to see the famous Mahatma Gandhi. Gandhiji still remained silent. As Gandhiji descended from . the train to a welcoming crowd of thousands, the man fell at his feet, begging for forgiveness. Gandhiji, of course, blessed and forgave him, telling him only that he should be more respectful of others, regardless of who they are. This is the spirit of yagna. This is the spirit of India that we must maintain in our hearts.

Another beautiful example of Gandhiji's humility, his selfless sacrifice for his country is how he "celebrated" his victory. When India won independence, when Gandhi was the hero of the country, he could have been in New Delhi receiving boundless honors and appreciation. However, he was not. He was not in New Delhi, nor was he in Bombay, nor in Calcutta. He was nowhere that would shower him with love and esteem. Rather, he was in East Bengal where Hindus and Muslims were fighting bitterly. He was not content to have "fulfilled his mission." If humans were still suffering, then he still had work to do. So, while the rest of the country celebrated, Gandhiji continued his tireless work to heal the wound between Hindus and Muslims. This is the spirit of sacrifice. This is the spirit of divinity.. Even when all external circumstances throw you to the center, you remain humble, you remain simple, you remember for whom your yagna was performed. Gandhi's yagna was for his country, not for his own fame.

Sacrifice for the principles of right living
However, his life was not only a sacrifice for Mother India. It was also a yagna of morality, of *dharma*, of ethics and

of truth. How easy it would have been to fight with weapons; how easy to kill the enemy. How easy to carry a gun to protect himself. Yet, the flames of Gandhi's yagna were fueled by non-violence. Wars throughout history had been won with weapons. Gandhi was devoted to proving that peace could only come through peace. People criticized him vehemently for refusing to take up arms; they claimed he was forfeiting India's fight for freedom. Yet, he simply kept pouring truth, piety, and *dharma* into the fire of his life yagna, and the flames rose in victory. This is the true meaning of yagna, for Gandhi sacrificed an easy-win (or at least a quick loss) for India by refusing to engage in armed warfare. He sacrificed his popularity; he sacrificed his status as a fighter. Yet, the truth prevails and he is remembered as one of the greatest leaders — both political and spiritual — that the world has ever known.

Sacrifice to God

Mahatma Gandhi's life was in service to God. His work for his country and his tenaciously held values were part and parcel of this complete sacrifice to the divine. The Gita was his closest companion, and his most trusted guide.

So many people today claim that their lives and their work are "God's." Yet, they use this as an excuse to lie, to cheat and even to kill. And, at the end it is clear that they merely used God's name in the service of themselves. Yet, Gandhiji was pure and his death is the clearest example. Due to his tenaciously held belief in *ahimsaa* and his true surrender to God, he refused to employ a bodyguard. Hence, he was gunned down on his way to a prayer meeting. As he breathed his last, there was no sign of fight, no break from his lifelong dedication to non-violence and to the divine.

He did not scream, "Who are you? How dare you? Somebody help me!!" Rather, the only words that escaped from his lips were "*He Ram, He Ram, He Ram.*" This is the spirit of yagna.

What can we learn ?

So many people come and go in this world. So many people become famous through valiant efforts to "make a name for themselves." Yet, how many of these people have really left lasting impressions or have really changed the course of history? Very few. When we depart this Earth, when we leave our bodies, what is it that remains? It is that which we have given to the world. It is that for which we have sacrificed. It is the love and the peace that our presence brought to those around us. Gandhiji's name will live eternally not only because he brought independence to India. He will be remembered forever and revered forever because of the *way* he brought peace, because of the message of his life.

When Gandhiji was in South Africa he was traveling by train and the conductor came and rudely told Gandhi to leave. "But, sir, I have a ticket," Gandhi replied. The conductor violently threw him from the train and yelled, "You do not deserve to ride on this train!" Gandhi, however, did not raise an arm in his defense. And today, does anyone know the name of the man who threw him from the train? Of course not. But, today the name of that train is "Mahatma Gandhi Train", and the name of the station is "Mahatma Gandhi Station"! That is the spirit of yagna.

Gandhi would not have wanted to be remembered only in history books. He would not want to be remembered only as the politician who led India to independence. He would want his message to live on; he would want his yagna to continue burning, to continue bringing light and warmth to all the world. In fact, when someone once asked him for a message, he replied, "my life is my message."

So, as we remember this Mahatma, this "great soul," let us take his message to heart. Let us live our lives as a sacrifice to world peace, as a sacrifice to our principles and as a sacrifice to God. Then, and only then, will our lives truly make a difference.

ॐ INDEPENDENCE AND FREEDOM – WHAT HAVE WE ACHIEVED?

Each year in August we celebrate the anniversary of Mother India's Independence. We revel in memories of Her strong yet non-violent victory over the British. We shout with pride, "Bharat Mata ki Jai!" This ardent pride in our culture and loyalty to our Mother Land and Mother tradition are the hallmarks of Indian people. Many historians have noted that India is the only country where the people were colonized so forcibly, for so many thousands of years, where the people lost neither the depth nor richness of their ancient culture; nor did the people's loyalty to their culture wane or dissipate.

Yet, as we celebrate this glorious holiday, as we rejoice in our hard-earned freedom, let us look beyond our external freedom to rule independently. Let us look at whether, internally, the people of India are truly free. Swarajya means "self-rule;" it means that we, the Indian people, have control over our own land, our own government and our own rules. So, we achieved outer swarajya; we achieved freedom from the British. But, have we achieved inner Swarajya? Do we, each of us, have control over ourselves? Are we truly free internally?

The chains used to be imposed by the British. They were overt and obvious. However, so many of us are still bound by chains, yet these chains are more subtle and insidious.

They are the chains of our attachments to worldly possessions; they are the chains of our craving to be more and more Western, thereby leading us to forsake the richness of our culture; they are the chains of corruption – both external and internal; they are the chains of desires for sensual fulfillment.

The chains of our attachments to worldly possessions and sensual pleasures keep us prisoners even more than the British imperial rule. When our focus in life is on attaining more and more wealth, more and more material objects, more and more prestige and fame, and more and more comforts then we must live within a set of rules even more limited than those imposed by the colonizers. We must forsake our family for our job. We must spend less and less time engaged in spiritual pursuits in order to "get ahead" at work. We must travel extensively, thereby weakening the bonds of family. But, most importantly, when we are focused on material success, or sensual pleasures we are not even free in our own minds. Check yourself. Sit quietly. What comes to you first? Is it God? Is it a passage from the scriptures? Is it a desire to go to temple? When we are committed primarily to material prosperity, our predominant thoughts tend to be those pertaining to our careers, our investments, our colleagues, our projects and our desires. These concerns trap us and prevent us from finding true freedom in life.

Yes, it is wonderful to be successful. It is wonderful to be prosperous. It is wonderful to be comfortable and to enjoy life. Even in our scriptures, Bhagwan Shri Krishna was a king who lived in a city of gold. However, it is the pre-occupation with the accumulation of more and more that binds us. It is the obsession with "success at all costs" which becomes our captor. In order to be truly free, we must loosen the chains of this attachment. We must perform our duties for God, and take whatever comes as prasad. However, we should never become slaves to our desires for possessions, because these desires can never be satiated, and they simply lead to our misery and bondage.

Another chain which, sadly, is enslaving many Indians today is the desire to be Western. The Western media – television, movies, commercials, magazines – have convinced the Indian people, especially our youth, that the keys to happiness lie in being as Western as possible. Thus, they chase after Western fashions, Western entertainment and Western lifestyles. However, although the West has a great deal to offer in terms of academic and professional excellence, it does NOT hold the keys to true peace, meaning and joy in life. These keys lie in the ancient, yet timeless, culture of India. They lie in the wisdom of our scriptures. They lie in our rich tradition. Thus, our youth (and now, unfortunately their parents as well) are trapped in a vicious cycle in which with each effort to become more and more Western they must forsake another piece of their Indian culture. Thus, although they are searching for deep and lasting happiness, they will find only superficial, temporary pleasure.

The key to breaking this chain lies in love and acceptance of Bharat Mata and Her culture. It lies in learning as much as we can – academically, professionally, technically, scientifically – from the West without abandoning our loyalty to our own value system and our own sanskaras. When our children can look at themselves and their friends and say, "I am proud to be Indian," then, and only then, will they truly be free.

We are also bound by the chains of corruption – corruption within our government and social systems, as well as corruption within our families and ourselves. Corruption in the government and our social systems is a problem which must be eradicated if India is ever to be a truly free nation. Freedom implies trust. Inherent in the meaning of true freedom is the ability to have faith in that system to which one adheres. If we require the people to pay heed to the government, (and if we require them to abide by the rules set out by the government), then we must, in turn, give them a government in which they can have faith. Otherwise, if we demand their loyalty and obedience to a system riddled by corruption and dishonesty, then are we any better than a colonizer?

However, it is not only corruption in the government which enslaves the people; the corruption within our own hearts can be even more insidious. Are we honest people? Are we righteous? Do we uphold the principles of dharma? We fought a long, arduous battle to win our right to freedom. Let us truly bask in this freedom, realizing the real richness of our values, ethics and sanskaras. The principles set forth in our scriptures are just as applicable to people living in modern Mumbai or Delhi as they were to people living thousands of years ago in the Himalayas. Let us not be bound by the chains of jealousy, anger and greed. These chains bind not only our hands but also our hearts. Instead, let us live lives of generosity, seva, love, purity and divinity. Then, our hearts, minds and souls will all be free.

Our country won independence 55 years ago. When will we win independence over ourselves? When will we be the ones to determine the path of our lives, rather than let that path be dictated by our desires, our attachments, our lust and our greed? God had given each one of us the veto power. We must simply exercise it. I always say, "We are not lightbulbs that can be switched on and off at the will of others." Yet, too frequently, we act like that. Too frequently, we let the rest of the world determine our state of mind, our choices and our values. Let us take our lives back into our own hands, and turn the reins over only to God. When our lives become surrendered to His service, to service for Bharat Mata and to service for dharma, then we will truly be free.

 CORPORAL PUNISHMENT

Corporal punishment is all too frequently used in homes and schools across the world. People seem to believe that children require physical and emotional violence in order to be "well-trained" or to be properly scolded for their bad behavior. This is, however, a tragic falsehood, and one that leads to nothing more than an escalation of violence in our society.

Violence leads to violence. Peace leads to peace. This is a truth that pertains to countries at war as well as to our youngest children. When we raise our voices, when we become angry and aggressive, so our children raise their voices and their fragile bodies flood with anger and aggression. We hope that by becoming aggressive, our children will become calm, repentant and defensive. This is not the way the world works, however. When we act with anger, we create an environment of anger in the home. This negative energy persists, like a toxic chemical, in the home long after the actual fight is over. Our children, at the most receptive time of life, are then breathing in air filled with violence, lack of control, and negativity. And we wonder why our world is becoming more violent each day...It is not such a mystery.

Additionally, when we hit our children (and this includes slap and spanks, which many people seem to believe do not count as "violence") we also lose their respect. Children are much more perceptive and insightful than we sometimes believe. As they watch us turn red with rage and then explode in verbal or physical attacks, they know we have lost control. They know we have no other methods by which to teach them. Their respect for us quickly diminishes. This, of course, pertains to teachers as well. It is so important for children to respect their teachers. How else can young, exuberant bodies sit still for so many hours each day? Yet, when they lose respect for us as people, they simultaneously lose respect for what we are teaching. There are so many important lessons to be learned in school, that we can not afford for the students to lose their respect for teachers. For some reason we seem to believe that if we punish them severely they will respect us. This is absurd. Sure, they will fear us. But respect and fear are not even related. We do not our children's (or our pupils') fear. We want their respect.

We complain that our children lie, that they hide from us, that they disrespect us. We ask why. Yet the answer is not a mystery. Children are like sponges, voraciously soaking up every aspect of the environment in which they live. If they live with lies, they will tell lies. If they live with disrespect, they will show disrespect. If they live in the vicious cycle of action/reaction they will only know how to act and react. If they live in a home in which there is neither tolerance nor understanding, they will learn to keep everything to themselves. However, if they live with patience, with love, with tolerance, with a tender touch of teaching, they will manifest patience, love, tenderness as well as learn the lessons we are trying to teach them.

The keys to divine children lie in changing the nature of how we — as parents and teachers — behave. We must never act in anger or frustration. We must wait until we have calmed down and then, gently and tenderly, explain things to the children. Then, and only then, can we be sure they are only getting the teaching they deserve, and not the brunt of our anger from the office or from the traffic on the way home. How many times have we had exasperating days and come home and taken it out on the children (or one our spouse who then, in turn, takes it out on the kids)? Too many. And what do the children learn from this? Nothing other than low self-esteem and insufficient tools for dealing with their own emotions.

So, the first thing to do wait until you are in a "teaching" mood, not a scolding mood. For children need not only the teaching, but they need the "touch." And that touch should be velvet, not violent. With a velvet touch and calm mind you can achieve anything with children. We should have "eye" communication. You should be able to simply look at them in a certain way and have them understand. There should never be the need to raise your voice.

Yet, I also understand that this is not easy. It is not easy to be calm when we are full of rage inside. It is not easy to use a velvet touch when our instinct is to hit.

Perhaps we say, "but I was hit by my parents and by my teachers. That is just the way it should be." Yet, we must be better than this. We must not fall into the trap of being like robots, unable to think critically. I, too, was slapped by my first Spiritual Master. He believed it was the way to teach. Sure, at the time I obeyed him. I feared him. But, I can see clearly now that that was not the way to teach me. I can see, in retrospect, how much more I learned through his silence or through his calm — and sometimes stern — words, than through his slaps.

Our scriptures say that a mother and father are enemies of their children unless they teach the children well, unless they fulfill their duties of imparting understanding and values. The scriptures say that these parents are enemies of their children unless they provide real education. Education does not mean simply dropping the children off at school each morning. It means ensuring that they are learning right from wrong, truth from falsehood, integrity from deception.

It reminds me of a story I heard once. There was a man who was caught stealing. As this was the last in a long string of thefts, the judge finally sentenced the man to death. When the court asked the man what his last wish was, the man replied, "to meet with my mother." Thus, as the court always tries to fulfill the last wish of dying men, the mother was called. Upon her arrival, her son touched her feet and then, suddenly, leaped up and bit her face, causing blood to rush out of her gaping wounds. Everyone was astonished. Why would a dying man viciously maim his own mother?

In explanation, the man replied, "If I am going to die, it is because of her. All that I have become is because of her. When I was a small boy and I used to steal things, I would bring them to her and she would praise me. She never taught me that stealing was wrong, she simply encouraged it. And when she was angry with me, she never explained to me what I had done wrong. She never sat me down and tenderly helped me understand. Instead, she would simply beat me or scream at me. In that way, I too learned violence instead of values. So, I wanted to show the world that if I have become a criminal worthy of death, it is because of who she was as a mother."

I do not tell you this story so that we may all simply blame our parents for our own weaknesses. Rather, I tell it to illustrate the crucial nature of the effect parents and teachers have on children.

The children are the future of the planet, and it is our responsibility to help them make that future a bright one. Will we lead the world toward violence, or will we lead it toward love? Will we instill the values of forgiveness in the future world leaders, or will we instill the values of retribution and vengeance? Will we lead it toward greater calmness or toward greater chaos? We must never take for granted the role we play in the future of the world, through what we teach our children.

STORIES

TO TEACH YOUR MIND
TOUCH YOUR HEART AND
UPLIFT YOUR SPIRIT

 # THE DANGER OF ANGER

There was once a young boy with a terrible temper. He used to speak harshly and get angry many times a day, at the slightest provocation. His wise father told him that every time he got angry he had to hammer a nail into the wood fence in the backyard. The first day the boy hammered 45 nails into the fence – practically his entire day was spent in the back yard. The next day, with his arm sore from hammering, he tried to get angry less. He hammered only 25 nails into the fence the second day. By the end of a few weeks, the boy proudly went to his dad and told him that he had not gotten angry at all that day.

So, the boy's father told him that now he could start removing the nails from the fence. There were 2 ways that nails could be removed: either if the boy could go an entire day without getting mad, or if the boy apologized sincerely to someone whom he had hurt through his anger.

So, the boy began to apologize to people whom he had wounded and he tried hard not to get angry. Slowly, slowly, the nails began to get pulled out of the fence. One day, the boy proudly went to his dad and told him that all the nails were out of the fence. He told his dad that his anger was "a thing of the past."

His dad then led the boy by the hand to the fence and

showed him how the fence was now riddled with holes. It was no longer the sturdy, strong fence it once had been. It was now weakened and damaged. Every time the wind blew strongly the fence swayed in the wind, for it was so full of holes that the breeze caused the fence to move.

"Do you see that?" the father asked the boy. "For you, anger is a thing of the past. This fence will never recover. Every time you get angry at someone it is like driving a nail into them. You may later remove the nail, but the hole is still there. The effect of your anger can not be removed."

In life sometimes it is easy to get angry, easy to yell, easy to hit those we love. We assuage our own consciences by saying, "He made me mad," or, "She made me hit her." But, whose hand is it really that hits? Whose mouth is it really that speaks harsh words?

We think, "It's no big deal. I said sorry." Or we say, "Oh, but that was yesterday. Today I've been nice." For us, it may be that easy. But remember the fence is still sitting there with a hole in it, even though you have moved on. If you hammer enough nails into someone, eventually they will be forever weakened, forever damaged. You can stab someone with a knife and then pull out the knife but the blood will continue to pour. "Sorry" does not stop the blood of wounds. It may pave the way to recovery, but the wound is still there.

The goal in life should be to be like water – a stone falls in and only causes a ripple for a moment. The "hole" in the water caused even by a large boulder does not last for more than a few seconds. When we get hit – verbally, physically or emotionally –we should be like the water. We should be able to just let the ripples flow and, within a few moments, it should look as though nothing happened.

However, unfortunately it is very difficult to be like the ocean. Very few people in the world are able to accomplish this task, for it is a task of great sadhana and vairagya (non-attachment). It is much more common that people are like fences – the holes you hammer into them stay with them for a lifetime. Children, especially, are like the wood fence. No matter how much they grow in life, no matter how wise they become or how old and strong they become, those holes are still there.

We must remember that our loved ones are like wood. Therefore, we must try to be very, very careful before we hammer holes into anyone, before we stab knives into anyone's heart...if there are too many holes, the fence will fall.

# THE MESSAGE OF THE BUDDHA

There is a beautiful story told of a disciple of Lord Buddha who wanted to publish a book of the teachings of Buddhism. So, he spent several years compiling the great wisdom of Lord Buddha and placing it in book form. Then, it was time for the task of raising enough money to publish the book. He went door to door to his friends and neighbors requesting help in bringing this project to fruition.

After he had collected enough funds, he was about to publish the book when a large cyclone hit a poor area of the country. Immediately, he sent all the funds to the disaster-struck region to help the victims.

Again, then, he underwent the task of collecting money to publish this important book. Again, his friends, relatives and colleagues helped him reach the goal. Then, an earthquake struck another area of the country, killing thousands. Again, the disciple sent all of his hard-earned funds to the region.

Several years passed during which he tried, with difficulty, to raise the funds a third time. However, people were not ready to keep giving for the same book. Thus, it took him quite some time to raise enough money to publish the book. No catastrophe struck and the book was published. On the inside cover of the book, beneath the title "Teachings of Lord Buddha" was written "Third Edition."

So many times in life we read spiritual teachings, we listen to lectures and katha, we say our prayers. However, do we actually implement these teachings in our life? The book was a "third edition" because the teachings of Buddhism include compassion, non-attachment and service to the poor. Thus, by donating the funds for the book to disaster-struck victims, the disciple was, actually, teaching and illustrating the word of the Buddha.

He knew that the word of the Buddha was to help those in need. Thus, it is even more illustrative of Buddhism to help the poor than to publish books.

In our lives, too, we must remember not only the words of the teachings, but also the true message of the teachings. We read the books, we listen to the lectures, but do we absorb the message? Sometimes we get so caught up in reading, hearing and reciting these teachings that we forget to live them!

Service to others is the true message, the true teaching, the true wisdom of spirituality.

 # BREAKING THROUGH OUR SHELL

There was once a man who noticed a beautifully woven cocoon on a tree outside his home. He carefully watched the cocoon every day in order to catch the first glimpse of the beautiful butterfly he knew would emerge. Finally, one day he saw a tiny hole in the cocoon which grew quickly as the hours passed. He sat watching the butterfly break her way out of the cocoon. However, suddenly he noticed that it seemed the butterfly had stopped making progress. The hole did not get any larger and the butterfly seemed to be stuck. The cocoon was bouncing up and down on the branch as the butterfly tried to squeeze herself, unsuccessfully, through the hole she had created.

The man watched in dismay as it seemed his butterfly would not be able to emerge. Finally, he went inside, took a small pair of scissors, and carefully cut the cocoon, allowing the butterfly to emerge easily. However, the butterfly immediately dropped to the ground instead of soaring gracefully into the sky as he imagined she would.

The man noticed that the butterfly's stomach was swollen and distended but her wings were small and shriveled, explaining her inability to fly. He assumed that after some time, the stomach would shrink and the wings would expand, and she would fly in her fullest glory. However, this was never to be.

The man didn't know that it was the very act of forcing her body through the tiny hole in the cocoon which would push all the fluid from her stomach into her wings. Without that external pressure, the stomach would always be swollen and the wings would always be shriveled.

In life, too frequently, we avoid the challenges, looking for the easy way out. We look for people who will "cut our cocoons," so that we never have to work and push our way through anything. However, little do we realize that it is going through those times of difficulty which prepare us for the road ahead. The obstacles in our path are God's way of making us able to fly. With every bit of pushing and struggling, our wings become fuller and fuller.

So frequently, people come to me and say, *"Oh, why has God given me so much strife. Why has He put so many obstacles in my path? Why is He punishing me?"* We must realize these are not punishments. Sure, karma plays a large role in what we receive in this lifetime, but even the things that seem like "bad" karma, are actually opportunities for growth. Even an extra small hole to squeeze through is actually an opportunity for our wings to expand to great lengths.

So, let us learn to take our challenges for what they are, rather than looking around for a "different" hole, or for someone with a pair of scissors. These things may help us quickly through the cocoon, but we will be unable to fly in life.

GOD'S WIFE

A small, impoverished boy was standing barefoot on the New York City streets, looking wistfully in the window of a shoe store. A well-dressed woman saw him and asked him, "Why are you looking so solemnly in this window?" The small boy looked up at her and replied, "I am asking God to please give me a pair of shoes."

The woman took the boy's small hand and led him into the shoe store, where she immediately asked the clerk for a bucket of warm water and 10 pairs of socks. Then, placing the boy's dirty feet into the water, she tenderly washed them and then put a pair of warm socks on him. Then, she told the clerk to bring shoes for the boy.

As they left the store, the boy's small feet now snugly in a pair of new shoes, he clenched the woman's hand and looked up into her eyes. "Are you God's wife?" he asked.

This story is not only a beautiful snippet from life in a big city. Rather it is a deep lesson about how to live our own lives. Instead of simply saying, "Oh, how sweet," and moving on, let us really take this story to heart.

How easy it is to pass by those less fortunate with a simple sigh of sympathy or with a token "aid," perhaps a coin or two tossed in their direction. These small gestures of empathy and charity make us feel like we are compassionate people who just live in an "unjust" world. However, is the homeless man helped by our sigh of disdain? Does the coin we hand him really make a difference? Are we really being compassionate, or are we just soothing our own consciences?

How much more difficult it is to really stop, take a moment out of our hectic lives and see what is needed. Yet, how much more divine that is. There are always places to be and things to do. If we wait until we are "free" in order to take care of others, the time will never come. Real divinity, real selflessness is giving when it is not necessarily convenient to give. It is giving according to the others' needs, not according to our own agenda and convenience.

The wealthy woman probably had some place else to be on that cold day in New York City. She could have easily looked the other way and continued on with her errands. But she didn't. That is what makes her special.

We tend to give decadently to ourselves and to our own families. We will pile gifts under Christmas trees until there is no room left. We will shower each other with new clothes, toys, and other merchandise on birthdays and anniversaries. No problem. We love each other and so we give gifts. This is fine. However, let us also remember, though, to extend that compassion and that love to others who really need it. Let us vow never to turn a blind eye on someone in need. Let us vow to use what God has given us to really serve His children. Let us live our lives as though we, too, are "God's wife."

 # SACRED DROPS OF BLOOD

There was once a very great sanyasi; he possessed the ability to transform people by his mere words. The sound of his voice carried listeners into the stillest, most peaceful meditation. But, he wanted to do more for the world. His vision was to help all of humanity, to be of service to all those he met, to heal the world on a massive scale. He prayed to God to give him the ability to save people's lives. "You can not save everyone; you can not be of service to everyone. Just keep speaking, keep chanting, keep writing, keep praying. In this way you will really heal," God said to him. But the saint was not persuaded. "Please, God, let me be of service – of direct service – to all. Let me save people's lives."

The sanyasi had performed so much tapasya and was so pure in his desire to help, that God granted him the boon of being able to save the life of anyone who came to him. He had simply to take a drop of his blood and place it on the patient's upper lip. Any ailment would be cured; any suffering would immediately be alleviated. The saint was exuberant; his dream had been fulfilled. Now he felt that he would really be able to save the world and to cure those who came to him.

The first day four people came. For each person, he simply pricked the tip of his finger with a needle and the blood came out. One small drop had such miraculous healing powers. That night, the selfless saint had a beaming smile on his face for those whom he had cured.

The next day, forty people came, having heard of his miraculous powers. For each he squeezed a small drop of blood from his finger and blessed them as he placed it on their upper lip. Each was instantly cured. Paralysis, leprosy, depression, anxiety – all disappeared with the simple drop of the sanyasi's blood. As word spread throughout the land, more and more people flocked to his healing magic. And the sanyasi was in bliss – here he was using his simple God-given blood to cure so many. He dispensed these drops freely – with no hesitation, no discrimination, no vacation. "I am in your service..." he would say.

Soon, thousands were flooding the simple ashram in which he lived; they were overflowing in the streets. The saint was dispensing the equivalent of cups of blood each day. But, he did not even notice. Such was his dedication and devotion to those whom he was curing. He sat, in meditative bliss, as he squeezed first his fingertip, then the veins in his arm to dispense blood to those in need.

It was not long before the sanyasi had to squeeze harder in order to coax the blood from his body. Soon, a mere needle prick was not a large enough opening; he needed small knives to pierce the prominent veins of his forearms and legs. From there, the blood flowed freely again, and all were relieved. However, soon, even those veins were no longer coursing with high volumes of healing nectar. They, too, were becoming drier and drier.

As his blood volume dropped each day, the sanyasi became weaker. The color drained from his once vibrant face. Darkness drew circles around his eyes. His voice, which previously had boomed, singing forth the divine glories of God, was now not much more than a whisper. But, the sanyasi was not worried. Those who loved him urged him to take rest, to take at least a break from giving blood, to let himself recuperate.

Although he listened with his ears and appreciated the concern, he could not stop pumping blood from his body. He would say, "I am in the service of the world...These people have come from so far...They have been waiting for so long...This man is an important minister, but he's suffering from pneumonia...I feel no pain. I feel no weakness. I feel only the joy of giving myself to others." Those who loved him could do nothing, other than watch the scores of people continue to pour in, continue to plead for "just one drop."

Soon, even the once succulent veins of his forearms would give no more blood. Even the largest, most abundant veins of his body held on selfishly to their sparse quantity of this life-giving fluid. But, the sanyasi was not deterred. "This is only a challenge. Only more tapasya to do," he would say. He ordered his servants to build a device which would squeeze harder than human hands were able to, a vice-like apparatus into which he could place a limb and have it milked completely of the blood inside.

Throughout this, the people kept coming. As word spread – in frantic whispers – that the saint was ill, that the blood was running dry, the people flocked even more frenetically. They pushed and trampled one another in an effort to get "just one drop." People, who perhaps had been postponing a visit until a later date, dropped everything and came running. "Please Maharajji," they would plead. "Please, just one drop. We have come from Madras, we have come from Nepal, we have come from London. My daughter has this horrible affliction on her face. My husband lost his arm in a car wreck. My son refuses to get married. Please Maharajji, please just one drop. Just one drop and then we'll go away so you can take rest." For each who came, the saint smiled as he placed a drop of blood on their upper lip.

The ocean of his blood soon became an arid desert. Where once his veins had flowed like copious rivers, they were now limp and desiccated

His devotees pleaded with him to stop; their tears of concern poured onto his holy feet. But, all he could see were needy, ailing people stretching out to the horizon, each one crying pitifully, "Please, Maharajji, just one drop."

When those who had flocked for blood realized that the sanyasi could give no more, they were un-deterred. "We will work the pumping machine," they screamed. And they stormed toward the saint, who sat peaceful, although nearly lifeless, draped only in his simple dhoti. But, the pumping machine was not powerful enough to pump water from a desert. So, they tied him up, the ropes cutting deep into his parched skin. And as some pulled the ropes tighter and tighter, others cut into his veins with knives (no longer small ones, but now the type used for butchering animals). "There must be another drop left. There must be," they cried furiously.

As his beloved devotees watched, the last drop of blood was cut from their great sanyasi, who had once overflowed with life, with vigor, with dynamism. Now he hung, still in the ropes which had tied him, lifeless and completely desiccated. However, they noticed, there was a smile on his limp and pallid face.

"Just five minutes," we plead. "Just step foot in my house to bless it...just take one meal at my home." It may not be physical blood we demand, but both our desperation and the effects on the saints is the same. "But, I've waited 5 years. But I've come from America. Please, Maharajji, just five minutes....but Maharajji, my daughter said she won't get married unless you are there...but, I can not go into surgery unless you come to the hospital...but it would mean so much to us if you could just come to our home for 10 minutes..."

When we go to visit a saint, rarely do we ask when he last took his meal or what his usual time for rest is. "It's only 5 minutes," we convince ourselves. "Just one drop, one drop of blood..." When we are blessed enough to have a saint at our home, rarely do we say to him, "Go to sleep. You must be tired. You have sat with people [or worked] all day long." Rather, we think "But, it's only once a year he comes," or "But this is the first time we've ever had him alone."

"Just one drop...just one drop and then we'll let you take rest."

Sure, it is only five minutes, or one hour, or one night. For us. But, we do not have the vision to see the streams of people, flooding out to the horizon, who will beg for "just five minutes," after we have had ours. Rarely, even do we lift our eyes to look.

"But," you may ask, "if the saint healed so many with his blood, why does it matter that he died? His purpose on Earth and his desire were to heal people. So, why does it matter that he lost his physical body in the meantime?"

The answer is that a doctor could have healed most of the physical ailments that came to him. Those suffering from emotional/psychological problems could probably have been helped had they put into practice that which he taught in his lectures. He did not need to give his actual blood to so many. But, it is easier to get the "instant cure," easier to let him place the blood on us than to make the trip to the doctor and take the medicine he prescribes, or to implement the necessary diet of less fat, less sugar, no meat, etc.

It is easier to be cured by someone than to cure ourselves. Somehow, when a saint speaks in public, giving instructions and messages publicly, we think that it pertains to everyone but us. "But I need to speak to him personally," we decide. "My problem is different." Rarely do we take a saint's "no" as "no." We know that if we plead harder, beg more desperately that they will give in, because they truly are in the service of humanity.

But, do we want to milk the blood from their bodies? Do we really want to be healed at their expense? Is that what love really is? We must realize that each of our demands, that each 5 minutes, each compulsory visit to a home, each one drop of blood, is only one of thousands more that he is selflessly giving to others. We must be careful to let him nourish himself such that his blood continues to flow. We must make a sincere effort to keep the life alive in these saints who would give their lives to us, without hesitation and without discrimination.

# GOLD UNDER BOULDERS

I heard a beautiful story of an ancient village where one day the villagers found a large boulder in the middle of their main pathway. The busy, rich businessmen and merchants had their servants carry them around it. Others simply turned back and returned in the direction from which they'd come, realizing that to try to pass was futile. Others gathered around the site of the boulder to criticize the King of the area for not taking better care of the roads. They stood by as the boulder obstructed passage on the road, condemning the King and his ministers for their laziness!

Finally, a peasant came by who was carrying a load of vegetables to sell in the market. He needed to pass the boulder, and so he calmly put down his heavy load and tried to push the boulder out of the way. However, the boulder was quite heavy. The peasant, though, just kept pushing from different angles and finally the boulder rolled. out of the road. As he bent down to pick up his load of vegetables, the peasant noticed something lying in the road where the boulder had been. It was a wallet filled with gold coins and a note from the king. The note said, "This reward is for he who has the commitment to move the boulder from the road."

So frequently in life we see that the "King" has thrown

obstacles in our path. Our natural instinct is to bypass them – using our influence or wealth – or to simply turn around and go a different path. Or, we give up the path altogether, seeing the obstacles as insurmountable. Perhaps we find ourselves criticizing life, circumstances, or the great "King" who is making our lives difficult. Yet, for he who has the commitment and dedication to conquer the obstacle, the rewards are great. Not only will the path be clear, but we will also become far richer (whether spiritually, mentally or financially) by having the tenacity to overcome the hurdles in our path.

Life is not always a clear path. If it were, we would learn very little. Rather, to test us, to teach us, to mold us and to make us stronger God challenges us. He – as the King of kings – places obstacles on our way. And, just like the king in the above story, He watches to see who will have the courage and the commitment to overcome these difficulties.

There is a beautiful saying in our scriptures which says:
Prarabhyate na khalu vighna bhayena nicheh
Prarabhya vighna vihata virmanti madhyah
Vighneh Punah punarapi prati-hanya manah
Prarabhya chottam-janah na parityajanti

This means that there are three types of people in the world. The first type, the lowest on the hierarchy of evolution toward God realization, contemplate the possibilities of failure before undertaking any task. Then, realizing that some obstacle will inevitably arise, and fearing the difficulties inherent in overcoming the obstacle, they decide not to act. Thus their lives pass in vain, and they perform no good deeds at all, for they are paralyzed by thoughts of hurdles that may arise.

The second type of people begin to perform good deeds but as soon as they encounter any difficulty, they turn back and relinquish the task. These people have good hearts and good intentions and they want to perform worthwhile deeds; however, they are unable to gather up the inner resources necessary to overcome any challenges. Thus, their lives also pass in vain, and although they have innumerable projects that were well-begun, they have not even one that was completed.

The third, and highest type of people are those who just keep going, no matter what obstacles they find in their path. They are so committed to completing their duties successfully that they steadfastly remove all hurdles from their way. They are entirely focused and centered on the ultimate goal, and they keep God's image in their mind, knowing that He is with them and that He will help them achieve their noble goals. These are the people who succeed, not only professionally in life, but also spiritually and mentally.

DIVINE ASSISTANCE

There was once a man who was a great devotee of God. He always believed that God would take care of him, regardless of the circumstances.

One day a great flood came to the town in which he lived. All the neighbors began evacuating their homes. However, this man was not worried. "God will take care of me," he assured himself.

Soon, the flood waters began to rise and water filled the first floor of the man's home. "No problem," he thought and moved to the second floor. At this time a boat came by, and the men in the boat shouted to him through the window, "Climb in, we'll save you."

"No," the man replied calmly. "That's all right. God will save me."

The men in the boat urged him to evacuate his home. "The waters are rising and rising," they cried. But, the man was undisturbed and sent them away, firm in his conviction that God would come through for him.

However, the rain continued and the waters rose and rose. The second and then third floor of his house filled with water. "No problem," he thought as he moved onto his rooftop. Sitting on the rooftop, wrapped in a rainjacket, the man saw a helicopter fly overhead. From the helicopter, a life preserver dropped down into the man's lap. "Grab on," the pilot yelled. "I'll save you."

But, the man would not grab on. "God will save me," he yelled back. "I don't need your life preserver." So, eventually, the helicopter flew away.

The flood rose and soon the man drowned.

When he entered Heaven, he said to God, "What happened? How could you let me drown? I thought you said you'd always save me. I had such faith in you."

God looked at the man sadly and said, "I sent you a boat; I sent you a helicopter. What else could I do?"

How many times in life do we avoid taking advantage of the situations which present themselves, instead holding tenaciously to our belief in karma, or fate, or divine will/ intervention? God will not always come to you draped in a saffron dhoti, flute in hand and whisk you away from unfortunate situations. He is more subtle, less obvious. He sends us the life preserver, but it is our choice whether to recognize it as "God sent" and grab on, or to cling to the belief that something better and easier will come along shortly.

Karma does not mean that we have no choice or no free will. It means we are handed a certain set of circumstances due to past lives, sanskaras, and so many other factors.

However, what we do with that set of circumstances is only partly determined by "fate;" the rest is determined by our own free will. For example, let's say our karma in this birth is to be given a cow. Okay, the cow comes from God – that is "His will." But, what we do with the cow is up to us. If we drink its milk and use its manure in our fields, then we will have radiant health and rich, fertile crops. However, if we eat the manure and spill the milk on the ground, our health will suffer and our crops will be weak and unproductive.

So many times we blame God for the situations in our lives, or we simply concede that it "must be our karma." However, if we are given the cow, is it our karma to be sick and have weak crops, or is that due to our own ignorance?

We must realize that everything comes from God, that everything is due to His will, and simultaneously we must understand that He has given us the power of discrimination and reasoning to make the right choices. It was the man's karma to have a flood destroy his home; it was God's kindness and compassion that sent the boat and helicopter; but it was the man's own ignorance and obstinacy that led him to drown.

So, when a flood comes in our lives, no problem. Perhaps that was meant to happen. BUT, when boats and helicopters come to save us, we must recognize them for what they are – God sent.

HEAVEN AND HELL

I have heard the story of a land called Hell. In this land the people are emaciated and famished. Yet, they are surrounded by bowls and bowls and platters and platters of luscious food. Why, then, are they ravished with hunger? Because, in this land called Hell, their arms cannot bend and thus they can not carry even one morsel of food from the plates to their mouths. Their hands grasp fresh breads, ripe fruits, spoonfuls of hot stews. But, in this land of Hell, their bodies can not receive the nourishment of this, for it can not reach their mouths. Their stick straight arms wave wildly in the air, desperately trying to figure out a way to carry the delicious food to their mouths.

The people in Hell cry out day and night. They futilely try to force their arms to bend. But the arms are rock solid straight. They try to eat directly with their mouths, but this is forbidden and they are beaten for it. So, they wither away eternity in this land of never-ending frustration, deprivation, and starvation.

I have also heard the story of a land called Heaven. In this land, as well, the people have only stick-straight arms. They, too, are surrounded by platters and bowls of scrumptious food which they cannot carry to their mouths. Yet, in Heaven, everyone is plump, well-fed, satisfied and joyful. Why is this? If you look carefully you will notice that, rather than obstinately trying to bend their own unbendable arms, they have simply learned to feed each other...

This is, truly, the only difference between Heaven and Hell...do we stubbornly fight the will of God? Do we wrestle unsuccessfully each day with situations that cannot be changed? Do we flail around, wildly and desperately, trying to change the unchangeable? Do we ignore our loved ones, our friends, our colleagues who could help us immeasurably? Do we insist on suffering in silence, never asking for a helping hand from those near us? Do we watch others suffering and withhold our own help because we are so caught up in our own distress? If so, then we are living in Hell.

Or, do we assess the situation, look around and see how the situation can be improved? Do we graciously offer our hands and our help to others? Do we accept others' help when we are in distress? Do we take joy in "feeding others"? Do we spend time nourishing other's bodies, minds and hearts? Do we let ourselves be fed with love? Do we allow others to nourish us, rather than thinking "I can do it myself?" If so, then we are living in Heaven.

Too often in the world I see people who are living in the Hell of their own isolation, in the Hell of their own frustration, in the Hell of their own determination to change the very nature of the world in which they live.

Families and friends gather together, frequently after many months of separation. I have seen innumerable situations in which family members and friends could so easily put an end to another's pain. Yet, they won't. They don't want to be the one to offer, "Here, let me feed you."

Or, in the opposite, but similar situation, I see so many people suffering who could be helped by their families and friends. Yet, they won't ask for help. They won't let others help them. They say, "I can do it myself." Their pride and ego will not allow them to say, "Will you feed me, please?" However, this is not the way it should be. When we gather with our loved ones, we must realize that it is they who can feed us when we are hungry, it is they who can alleviate our suffering, it is their love which will turn our lives from Hell to Heaven.

But, we must be willing to see the situation as it stands. If our arms are unbendable, we must accept that they are unbendable and then look for other ways to solve the problem. If we keep trying to change the unchangeable - in ourselves, in others or in the world - we will forever be frustrated and hungry - not only in the body, but also in the heart and in the soul.

So when families and friends gather together, if you see someone suffering, be the first to offer your help. Put aside any grudges or complaints or judgments. Simply offer your hand in assistance. And, if you are in distress, ask for help. These are your closest family and friends. Put aside your ego and pride. See how they can help you and ask for that. Then, as you feed them and as they feed you, your lives will change from Hell to Heaven.

A NEEDLE TO HEAVEN

Once, Shri Gurunanak Devji Maharaj, the founder of Sikhism and a very great saint, was on a pilgrimage. This was approximately 500 years ago, and the saint would travel by foot, freely dispensing wisdom, guidance and blessings to thousands of people. Along his way, a very rich man invited Gurunanak Devji to his home for the night. This home would be more aptly called a palace. There was marble and gold everywhere; expensive horses and carriages; dozens of sumptuous foods served out of sterling silver dishes. Tokens of the man's success abounded.

A truly great saint is always thinking about how to help us grow spiritually, how to uplift us, how to turn our minds and hearts to God. Gurunanak Devji Maharaj was such a saint. Additionally, a saint will never take anything without repaying the giver in some way. So, when he left the rich man's home, he handed the man a small sewing needle. "Hold on to this for me. I will take it back when I next see you," the saint said to the man.

Later, when the man told his wife what had happened, she was furious. "How could you have taken something that belongs to a saint? What happens if he dies before he sees you again?" It is considered a great sin to keep something belonging to a saint or to be in a saint's debt. This is why the rich man's wife was so angry. She told her husband, "You can not take the needle with you to Heaven when you die. So, if he dies first, you will never be able to give it back to him. Go now. Return the needle immediately!" So the man set out after the saint.

When he found Shri Gurunanak Devji, he handed him the needle and said, "Guruji, I can not bear the thought that if you should die, I would have no way of returning your needle to you. It is not as though I could take it with me when I die and then give it back to you in Heaven. I cannot. So, please take it now."

The saint smiled, took his needle, and looked deep into the rich man's eyes. "You are right. You cannot take this needle with you when you die. But, if you cannot even take this tiny needle, how do you think you will take all your possessions and wealth? That, too, must stay behind when you go. You can not even leave this Earth with a tiny needle, let alone a palace full of wealth."

"Oh my God. You are right." The man became white as a sheet. "All my life I have struggled for things that are as transitory as this body. I have sweat and slaved and forsaken my family in favor of acquiring more and more wealth. Yet, if God takes me tomorrow, I will lose it all in a breath. And, I have acquired nothing that will last. I have not done good deeds for others; I have not practiced sadhana; I have not served the world."

When he returned home, he immediately sold all his possessions - except the most basic necessities - donated all the millions of rupees to the poor, and devoted the rest of his life to God and the world. And do you know what? As he lay on his death-bed in the small, simple house with his wife and family by his side, he said, "I am far richer today than I was 30 years ago when Shri Gurunanak Devji came to my home."

What can we learn from this wise saint? His message is as apt and valuable in America and the West today as it was in the rural villages of India centuries ago. We come into this world with nothing but the love of our parents; we leave this world with nothing but the love we have created. All material things we acquire we must leave behind. I have never seen a rich man, a sports-star, a movie actress, a businessman, a doctor, a fashion model, or even the president ride to Heaven in a Mercedes, carrying a basket filled with luscious snacks. No, we leave this Earth alone. We cannot take our car, or our favorite clothes, or our finest china, not even one cent. All we can take is the karma of this life and the knowledge that we have spent this life in service, that the world is a better place because we lived.

HALF A SHAWL

A wealthy man is walking back to his home on a cold, windy, winter night. On his way he meets a beggar who is clad in nothing but a thin cloth. The beggar beseeches the rich man, **"Please, sir, give me your shawl. Otherwise I fear I will not make it through the cold tonight."** The rich man is also a pious man, a devoted man.

However, he still has a few blocks to walk to his home. He does not want to suffer during those few blocks without a shawl. Yet, his heart is pulled by the poor man and he knows that one must always help those in need. So, he decides that the best solution is to give half of his shawl to the poor man, and he will keep the other half. So, he cuts the shawl in half, wraps himself in one half and gives the other to the homeless man.

That night as the wealthy man sleeps, Lord Krishna comes to him in a dream. In the dream, it is winter and Lord Krishna is shivering, wrapped only in half of a shawl. "Lord, why are you wearing only half a shawl?" Lord Krishna replies, "Because that is all you gave me."

Our scriptures say that God comes in many forms. Frequently He comes to us in the guise of someone in need – an orphan, a homeless beggar. That is why our scriptures say to look on everyone, whether it is a prostitute, a crippled man, a dirty child or a crook as divine. It is easy to see God in His glorious, beautiful form. It is easy to adorn the temple deity with fine clothes and sandlewood tilak and to cook for Him with love. It is easy to sacrifice our own needs while we do the seva of a revered saint. It is such more difficult to extend the same love and selflessness to those in whom we don't see the obvious embodiment of the divine.

However, that is the task; that is the divine challenge. Our vision is limited. We see only on the surface. We see only the outer manifestations of what we perceive to be either holiness or lowliness. And we make our judgments based on these faulty perceptions. We give to those whom we deem worthy; we give as much as we decide the other needs. This is our mistake.

So, we must learn to cultivate divine vision. We must pray for the sight that shows us God in everyone and in everything. Who would even hesitate before offering God all we have and all we are? No one. In fact, our tradition is based on the very idea that everything we are and everything we do is for God. In yagna we say Idam namamah. "Not for me, but for you." Before we eat, we offer prasad to Bhagwan. We will not take food until He has first been served.

So, as our world is flooded with poverty, with violence, with hunger, with homelessness with destitution, let us open not only our two physical eyes, but let us also open our third eye, the divine eye. Let this eye show us God's existence in everyone, and let us serve others and treat others just as though they were Lord Krishna Himself who had come to us for assistance. Then, and only then, can we obliterate the distress in the world.

# LOVE, SUCCESS AND WEALTH

A young woman heard a knock on her door one day. When she went to open it, she found an old man on her door step. "Come in, come in," she said. The man asked, "Is your husband home?" The woman explained that her husband was not home, but the man was welcome to come inside anyway.

He refused, however. "I am here with my two friends," pointing to two elderly men waiting in the front yard. "However, we will wait outside until your husband returns."

That evening as soon as the husband came home, his wife told him what had happened. "Quick, quick, call them inside," the husband exclaimed. "We cannot leave old men standing in the cold outside."

So, the woman went outside and beckoned the men in. One of them rose and said, "Ma'am, we actually cannot all three come in. You see, I am Love, and with me are Success and Wealth. Only one of us can enter your home. Please, go and ask your husband which of us he would like in the home." So, the woman went and — relaying the story to her husband — said, "I think we should invite Success in. Then, you will get the promotion you've been waiting for and we will become more prosperous."

However, the husband thought and said, "But, Honey, I only want the promotion so we can be rich. If we invite Wealth into our home, then it won't matter if I get the promotion, because we will already be rich. I think Wealth is a better choice."

Their daughter then quietly spoke, "Mom, Dad. Let us bring Love into the home. If we have Love with us, then we won't care so much about Success or Wealth. We will be rich on the inside."

Her parents thought for a moment and finally acquiesced to their daughter's wish. So, the woman went outside and – addressing the man who had introduced himself as Love — said, "Okay, we have decided. You can come inside." So, Love took a step forward and began to walk toward the house. As he passed through the doorway, the woman noticed the other two men following. "Wait," she exclaimed. "We have chosen Love. You said that only one could come inside."

Love then paused and explained gently, "If you had chosen either Success or Wealth he would have had to enter alone. However, wherever Love goes, Success and Wealth always follow."

If you ask most parents what their concerns are regarding their children, you'll hear "I want him to get into a good university. I want her to get a good job and be successful." Time and energy are therefore expended in pushing the child academically, encouraging the child to excel, punishing or reprimanding the child for less than superb performance. Yet, a degree from a top university, a well paying job, a lucrative career — these are not the true marks of "success" in life.

True success comes when we are fulfilled, joyful, peaceful and prosperous – both internally and externally. So, fill your homes with love — love for God, love for each other, love for the community, love for all of humanity. Then, through that love, through that divine connection, all else will automatically follow. It is when we focus only on Success or Wealth that we find ourselves rich but not fulfilled, successful but not content.

 # LOYALTY OF THE BIRDS

A long time ago, in the times when animals and man and plants still spoke the same language, there was a large fire that threatened to burn down many, many acres of forest. Flames whipped through the ground, devouring small shrubs, bushes, flowers and grass-lands. All the animals scampered for safety. Squirrels climbed high in the trees, frogs hopped quickly to lily pads in the middle of ponds, deer ran briskly to higher ground, birds flew to safety. As the fire raged, the billowing flames became more and more ominous, engulfing more and more of the forest. The waters of the pond began to boil, and the frogs hopped desperately from lily pad to lily pad.

Soon the rising flames began to envelop even the oldest, sturdiest, densest trees, consuming them from the inside out. Squirrels hopped and monkeys swung from branch to branch, tree to tree, trying feverishly to escape the fury and momentum of the fire.

High in one tree sat two birds, and they neither cried with fear nor attempted to fly to safety. When the forest ranger, clothed in a fire proof suit and attempting to ensure the safety of as many animals as possible, saw them he became frantic. "Fly away," he cried. "Go...shoo...fly." He yelled as loudly as he could, hoping to startle them into flight.

Yet they remained still, unwavering, complacent. The ranger picked up branches and began to throw them into the tree. "Fly away....Go! Go!" he beseeched them. But the birds would not budge.

Finally, the ranger looked up and cried, "The forest is burning. This tree will be nothing but ashes in a few hours. You will die for sure. Why in the world won't you fly away?"

After many moments of silence one of the birds spoke. "We have lived our lives in this tree. She has given us branches on which to build our nests and raise our young. She has given us fruit to eat and worms to feed to our babies. Her leaves capture the moisture each night, and in the morning she has let us suck on them for water. In the summer, she has blocked the sun and provided us with shade. In the winter, she has caught the snow herself, so it would not fall on us. As the wind blows through her leaves, she has sung to us. She has let us fly quickly to her highest branches to escape the tigers or other animals who would eat us. We know she will burn. If there were anything we could do to save her, we would do it. But, as much as we have tried to think of something, we realize we are helpless. There is nothing we can do. However, we will not leave her now.

"Our whole lives, and our parents' lives and our grandparents' lives, she has stood beside us, never flinching, never failing to provide us with anything we could need. How, in this most dire moment, could we abandon her? We may not be able to save her, but we will not let her die alone. That is why we stay. She will die, and we will die, but she will not leave us and we will not leave her."

We are so quick in life to switch loyalties - from one teacher to another, from one spouse to another, from one way of being to another. Our hearts are fickle. We will remain loyal as long as it serves us to do so, as long as we, too, benefit from the loyalty. But, is that really devotion? There is a reason that wedding vows include the phrase "for richer and for poorer, in sickness and in health."

It is very easy to be attached to someone who is healthy, happy and prosperous. It is more difficult to remain with someone who is sick, depressed and indigent. It is even more difficult to maintain the devotion when it may bring what looks like harm to you. I say "looks like harm" because the loss of your faith actually is much more damaging to your soul than any of these other superficial "catastrophes."

Pure, single-minded devotion is one of the most beautiful things on Earth. It is, in fact, the path of Bhakti. Yet, how many of us are really able to maintain this? Usually, we love God and have faith in Him when all is wonderful. It is more difficult to believe in a Divine Plan when that Plan causes agony. Please know, though, that it is at this time that your faith is most important. For, these are really the lessons of life. This is real spirituality. Spirituality is not about being where and with whom you are most comfortable. It is keeping the fire of your loyalty burning regardless of how much water is being poured on the flames.

This is the beauty of the birds. They realized there was nothing they could do to keep the fire away from their tree. So, they calmly and faithfully waited out God's plan. This sort of devotion may be seen as blind; it may be viewed as childish. Yet, those views are from a modern, Western standpoint which can only see devotion and loyalty as means to another end. However, they are ends in and of themselves.

Their simple and pure loyalty is going to carry these birds' souls to Heaven more than anything they would be able to accomplish with their remaining years, if they had forsaken their "mother" tree.

 # THE POWER OF LOVE

I heard a beautiful story of a college professor in New York who gave his business-economy students the assignment of going into the slums and finding 10 children each to interview. Then, the university students had to prepare reports on each of the 10 children they had interviewed. The final item of the assignment was for the students to rate each child's chance of success in the world.

So, the students all completed their assignments. With 20 students in the class, the professor ended up with 200 papers on 200 different children living in the slums. Every single report ended with the last question of "What are this child's chances of success in the world?" Each had the same answer: "This child has no chance."

Twenty or thirty years later, another professor at the same college came upon these 200 old reports in the economy department's filing cabinets. He thought it would be interesting to see whether all 200 children had really turned out to be victims of their impoverished, crime-ridden upbringings.

Amazingly, over 90% of the children who had "no chance" had turned out to be successful doctors, lawyers or professionals. The professor was astonished and went to each one to ask what had helped him or her become a success. Every single respondent (now they were middle aged) said, "Well, there was this one teacher I had who changed my life and gave me the ability to succeed."

The professor finally found this one teacher who had changed the lives of all the children. When he found her, she was past ninety and very frail. He asked her how she had possibly taken these impoverished children who had no chance of success in the world and turned more than 90% of them into successful professionals. The old woman looked at the professor very simply, smiled and said, "I just loved those children."

The power of love is enough to give hope to the hopeless, enough to turn failures into successes, enough to make lives worth living.

The teacher had not done any special program, nor had she taught the children any special skills. None of them recalled a particular lesson, activity or project. Rather, the simple fact that she loved them and believed in them was enough to change their lives.

We all have this power to transform not only ourselves, but others as well. Yet, do we use it? Do we take the divine gift of love in our hearts and use it as much as possible, to help as many as we can?

The message of Bhagwan Shri Krishna is, "Love, Love and Love all." From the moment He was 6 days old, He had enemies. So many demons and asuras came to kill Him. But what did He do? Did He fight them with anger? Did

He hate them? Did He send them forever to Hell? No. He granted them all liberation.

Wherever Bhagwan Krishna went — whether it was to palaces, to the simple hut of Vidurji, to the gardens of Vrindavan — He brought only His divine love. His divine love changed not only the lives of all those who met Him during His physical presence on Earth, but the ever-present love He continues to shower upon us change all who open their hearts to it.

Let us take to heart His divine message of
"Love All, Hate None. Heal All, Hurt None."

God has given us a special ability to touch others with our smiles, to change a life with a simple warm embrace, to bring meaning to the lives of others by our love. We must use this divine gift and never let it go in vain.

Flowers blossom under the warm rays of the sun, and the flowers of our lives — our children, our families, and all those around us — will blossom only under the warm rays of our love.

If we learn how to love others, really, truly love them, not for who we want them to be, but rather for who they are — for the perfect souls that God has created — then we have learned one of the greatest lessons of life.

ONLY YOU

There once lived a king, but he was not just any king. He was one of those kings who was so important, so powerful that history books will talk about him forever. This king ruled an area bigger than the land we now call America. His territory extended from sea to sea, across mountain ranges and deserts, through the jungle. No one knows how many subjects he had, because there were too many to count. People used to say that if you put all his money together, in one place, it would fill the oceans.

This king was the most powerful man the world had ever seen. Anything he commanded happened instantly. They tell the story that one time in the middle of winter, the king was craving mangoes. But, it was winter, and as you know the trees only give mangoes in the summer. However, this king was so powerful that when the mango trees heard he wanted their fruit, they began to produce huge, beautiful mangoes. The snow was washed off, and the king had sweet mango in December.

Being such a powerful king of such a large region, he had to travel quite a bit. And travel in those days was not as easy as it is today. There were no trains or airplanes. The king traveled by carriage, or it is more correct to say, he traveled with an army of carriages. And, because travel was so slow and difficult, he was frequently gone for long periods of time.

One time, he had been away for many months, visiting the farthest reaches of his kingdom, ensuring that everyone was happy, that everyone was taken care of. For, even though he was so rich and so powerful and had more subjects and money than one could count, he had a very pure heart and was very dedicated to all of his subjects. When he was about to return home, he sent letters to all of his queens (in those days kings had many, many queens). In the letters he asked if there was anything they would like, any special gift he could bring them from far away. Of course, he always returned with carriages collapsing under the weight of so many gifts for his family, but he wanted to know if they had any special requests.

Each queen sent a list back to the king. "Bring me silk sarees, lined with gold...bring me diamonds, fresh out of the Earth....bring me pearls from the depths of the sea...." However, while all of the other queens sent long lists, one queen sent only a piece of paper with "1" written on it. The king was baffled, for even though he was very pure and very devoted, he was not always very smart. He turned to his chief minister and said, "This queen is stupid. I knew when I married her that she was stupid. Everyone else sent a list of gifts they want. This queen writes only '1' on the paper. What is '1'?"

The chief minister was very wise; he was a true man of God, and he could see people's hearts. He laid his hand on the king's shoulder. "No, no." He said. "The '1' means 'only you.' She is saying that she only wants you. Everyone else wants jewels and sarees and silks. When this queen writes

'1' she is saying that you are number one. That you are all she wants. If you are there, with her, everything is there. In your presence, she wants nothing, needs nothing. And if you are not there, nothing can fill the hole left by your absence - not sarees, not diamonds, not jewels. If you are not there for whom will she wear the sarees? For whom will she wear the silks, the diamonds? What is the point of all these things if you are not there? Where you are, everything is. So, she wants you to bring yourself to her, and nothing else."

The king was silent. "Oh," he whispered, trembling. For now he understood. His whole life people had wanted him for what he had, for what he could do for them, what he could bring to them. He could bring wealth, he could bring possessions, he could bring health (for he had all the best doctors), he could bring grace and blessings (in those days, people believed that kings carried divine powers). But, no one had ever wanted only him, just for him. No one had ever wanted only his presence, even if it carried none of the other gifts.

Immediately, he sent his servants to fill the orders on the lists sent by the other queens; he sent his messengers to deliver those orders. And he, himself, went to the queen. When he saw her, his eyes locked with hers. Their tears seemed to flow together. Their souls seemed to embrace, although their bodies were still many feet apart. He moved slowly, almost as though floating, toward her. And he took her in his arms and held her. "You are the only one who has ever really loved me. The others thought they loved me. But, they loved me for what I brought to them. They loved me for how they felt when they were with me. They loved me for what I symbolized. And you love me only for me."

And the king stayed there, forever, with the queen. Because of its purity, their love just grew and grew, and it showered everything near them with light and joy. Everything in their presence flourished and blossomed. People talked far and wide about how the flowers in their garden were brighter, bigger, more alive than flowers anywhere else, how the birds all seemed to stay close to the castle. Even in winter when all the other birds flew to warmer ground and the land became silent, the birds at this castle stayed, and sang their blissful songs all year long. Even on cloudy days, there was always a break in the clouds big enough to ensure that the sun could shine on this castle.

And the king became even more rich, and even more powerful - although if you asked him, he would not have even noticed; he was too busy serving his subjects, serving God and loving his queen. And their love and light was so strong that it radiated to the farthest reaches of the kingdom, bringing joy and peace to all the creatures of the land, from sea to sea, across mountain ranges and deserts, through the jungles.

So many times we become completely convinced that having this or doing that or going there will bring us happiness. "If only I had more of this," we say. Children are famous for this, but perhaps they are actually only more vocal. We watch TV, we see movies, we see advertisements. The message in all of these is "Buy this, and then you will be happy." Sure the "happiness" takes different forms: some products bring happiness through beauty, others bring it through success, others bring it through the right foods. But, the message is the same: own this and you will be happy.

God is kind; God is giving. And we are His children. So, naturally, He will frequently give us what we ask for.

But, when we ask for these things, aren't we saying to God, "I don't really need you, I only need this possession. Your only purpose is to bring me the possession?" If, however, we have God in our lives, we have everything. Do you think that when the King himself goes to the queen's palace, all his messengers and servants, all his possessions don't come with him? Of course they do. Everything goes with the king. Where the king is, everything is.

God is the supreme king. The king of our lives. Where He is, everything is. Let us not lose sight of what it is we really need to be happy.

ॐ SERVICE TO OTHERS IS THE BEST MEDICINE

There is a beautiful story of a princess who was suffering from an undiagnosable illness. She lay in bed, listless, unable to walk or to exert herself at all. She had lost all appetite and her parents feared she would soon perish. Her father, the King, called in all the top doctors and medical specialists, but none could either diagnose or cure the young princess. They gave her allopathic, homeopathic, and ayurvedic medicines. They gave her pills, compresses, powders, massages and mineral baths. Nothing made even a dent in the princess's condition. She continued to lay, limp and mute, on her bed, staring blankly at the ceiling above her.

Finally, in desperation, the King called a revered holy man, a saint who was worshipped throughout the kingdom as having divine knowledge and powers. As soon as the sage saw the princess, he understood exactly what was wrong. "Pick her up and place her in the carriage," he ordered. The King refused. "How can you take this weak, fragile being outside in the carriage?"

Yet, the saint insisted. "If you do not follow my orders, your daughter may not recover. Wrap her warmly if you like and place her in the carriage. We will travel alone." The King had no choice; his options were exhausted and none had borne any fruit. He could only pray that the holy man knew what he was doing.

So the princess was wrapped in the warmest shawls and gingerly placed — supported by numerous feather pillows — in the King's carriage. The holy man got in beside her and instructed the driver where to go. He explained to the princess as they traveled, "I have a few urgent jobs to take care of on our way. You can accompany me." They soon stopped in a poor area on the outskirts of the Kingdom. The sage stepped down from the carriage, carrying large sacks filled with clothing and food. He walked house to house, delivering bags of rice, lentils, wheat to the impoverished villagers.

Soon, he returned to the carriage to find— as he had expected — the princess sitting up straight in her seat, peering eagerly over the side of the carriage. They drove a little ways, and again the sage stopped the carriage in another poor, rural village outside the wealthy kingdom. "I need your help in this village. There is too much for me to carry," he told the princess. She barely needed the help of his hand to get down from the carriage.

The sage carried the heavy bag and gave the princess the task of handing the food items and wool sweaters to the grateful villagers. At the first house, she walked slowly, delicately, and meekly put her hand in the large sack to take out the bags of rice and lentils.

However, by the third house she was striding confidently down the path, and by the fifth house she was picking up the young children to hold them in her arms. As they walked back to the carriage, she insisted on helping the saint carry the sacks of food, and she did not need any assistance to get back up into the carriage. Her cheeks were rosy; there was a beautiful, radiant smile on her face and a glow in her eyes.

Upon returning to the kingdom, three short hours after leaving, the princess nearly jumped out of the carriage and skipped up the steps to the castle! The King was amazed! How had the saint cured his daughter so completely, in such a short time?

The saint explained, "Your daughter was suffering from a lack of meaning in life. She was suffering from the disease of being spoiled and having every whim gratified. She was ill from a life being lived in vain. A journey to the poorest of the poor, a few hours of giving rather than taking, the experience of service and selflessness are the only possible cures."

Thereafter, the princess traveled twice each week with the saint, back into the poor villages, distributing food, clothing and other necessary supplies. She used her position as princess to help improve the living conditions of all those who lived in poverty. She dedicated herself to helping all those in need.

And she never suffered from a day of listlessness again...

Every day people in the West go out, go to work, earn money and become more prosperous. Yet, at the end of the day, when they return home, they are not happy. What is the true secret to internal peace and everlasting joy? I always tell people, *"Be God conscious, not glamour conscious."* Have Him in the center of your lives and you will find peace, happiness, meaning and joy.

However, it is difficult frequently to know HOW to implement the teaching of God in daily life. Yes, we should go to temple. Yes, we must chant His name (any name which appeals to us — whether it is Krishna, Rama, Jesus, Allah or Adonai). Yes, we must read from His holy words. Yes, we must pray to Him and offer our lives to Him.

However, what else can we do, so many people ask, to really become aware of God — full of God consciousness — in our daily lives? *We can serve His people!* Through service of the poorest of the poor we come closest to God. It is easy to see the divine in holy people, easy to serve those who look pious, proper and beautiful. But, the spiritual challenge is to see the divine in all, to serve all — from the highest King to the sickest leper — as though they are manifestations of God.

Through this selfless service, we not only benefit those whom we are serving, but we also benefit ourselves immeasurably. Our hearts fill with joy, with peace and with love. Our lives become full of meaning.

ॐ SHAKE IT OFF AND STEP UP

There is a story of a farmer who had an old mule. One day the mule fell into the farmer's empty, dry well. As the mule cried for help, the farmer assessed the situation. Although the mule had served the farmer faithfully for many years, the farmer decided that neither the mule nor the well was worth the trouble. So, he decided that instead of bothering to lift the heavy mule from the well, he would simply bury him in there. The farmer called his friend and together they began to shovel dirt into the open well.

When the first shovelful of dirt hit the mule he panicked. "What is this?" he thought. When the second shovelful hit him, he began to cry. "How could the farmer do this to me?" he wondered. When the third shovelful hit him, he realized the plan. However, the mule decided that he would not allow himself to be buried alive. As each shovelful hit fell upon his back, he rallied himself to "shake it off and step up." As shovelful after shovelful of dirt hit him on his back, and as he felt dejected and pained, he continued to chant to himself, "shake it off and step up." This he did, shovelful after shovelful, until – as the dirt reached the top of the well – the mule triumphantly walked out of what would have been his tomb.

If the farmer had not decided to kill the mule, the mule would never have survived. Ironically, it was the dirt which was meant to end the mule's life that actually ended up saving him, simply due to the way in which the mule handled the situation.

In life, sometimes we feel as though the world is "throwing blows at us." We feel shattered and broken. We feel as though we are being "buried alive." Perhaps someone is actually trying to injure us; or perhaps we are simply stuck in a difficult situation. Either way, we have two choices. We can either succumb to the onslaught and allow ourselves to be buried, or we can "shake it off and step up." The latter is surely a more difficult path. It requires resolution, will to survive, fortitude and faith. But, in the end, it is the path that will lead to our triumph. If we continue to "shake off" whatever hits us in life, and we continue to "step up" and rise above any situation, then we, too, will always be victorious and our lives will be successful and joyful.

# WE ARE ONLY HIS TOOLS

A few years ago the United Nations was having its 50th Anniversary Golden Jubilee celebration. World leaders - religious, political, social - were gathered together to commemorate this special anniversary. Numerous renowned people gave speeches -- on the global significance of the UN, on the importance of fostering inter-ethnic harmony, on how to curtail the insidious trafficking of drugs, on the necessity of preserving and protecting our rapidly diminishing natural resources.

Each was allotted a short period of time in which to speak. Most were given 3 minutes; some were given 5 minutes. The most important delegates were allotted 7 minutes. Time was watched carefully. Note cards were held up, alerting the speaker that he or she had 3 minutes left, then 2 minutes, then 1 minute.

The name Dada J.P. Vaswani was called, and an old Indian saint, clad only in scant saffron robes, walked slowly, yet purposefully and unwavering to the podium. As he spoke, silence descended upon the room. While most speeches were read from notecards, or were the product of careful and deliberate editing, his words seemed to speak themselves. Dadaji was given 5 minutes to speak. However, as the organizers held up signs that read, "2 minutes left," then "1 minute left," he showed no signs of winding up his talk. The signs then read, "30 seconds left," then "Finished!!!" However, the saint was in such ecstasy, he was so impassioned with the words that were effortlessly flowing from his mouth, that he seemed not to even notice the signs.

At first the organizers were noticeably restless and anxious. After all, there were so many other people to speak, so many other segments of this important function. How to get this saint to step down from the podium? However, as he continued, his words were like a lullaby. Even the anxious organizers became still and peaceful, mesmerized by the quality of his words and his tone. The hall - filled with an audience of thousands - was as quiet as if it were empty. Dadaji spoke for 25 minutes, an unprecedented amount of time.

When he concluded, the silence of the auditorium broke like thunder into a clamorous standing ovation. No one who was present was unchanged. The saint's words had reached not only minds, not only hearts, but also souls. He was flooded with accolades and tear-streaked faces as he descended from the stage. "Oh Dadaji, your speech was incredible. So inspiring. So uplifting. It was just wonderful." Everyone wanted to praise this gray-haired yet seemingly ageless Indian saint. After one man took Dadaji's hands and gave particularly effusive praise, the saint looked sweetly into his eyes and replied, "Yes, it was wonderful. I was also listening."

"I was also listening." "I was also listening." This should be our mantra. For, it is not we who speak. It is He who speaks, although we like to take the credit. How easy it would have been for Dadaji to have simply replied, "Oh, yes, I know my speech was good. I spent days preparing it." Or "Yes. I'm a very good speaker, aren't I?" However, he is a true man of God. He knows from where his words come. He knows whose words flow through his mouth. Those who are the true inspirations, who are the true teachers of this world, are actually simply channels. They are not the ones who spend lifetimes refining their tenaciously held beliefs and then impose these upon others. Rather, they simply open up the channels inside them and let God flow into their hearts and through their mouths or their pens. We are all here as tools for His work, as expressions of His love. Let us realize that; let us break the dams within us, so the river of His work and His message can flow ceaselessly through us.

WHO IS HANDICAPPED?

Across the world there is a wonderful organization called the Special Olympics. This foundation sponsors "Olympics" for people who are physically and/or mentally handicapped. These are people who may be suffering from anything ranging from partial paralysis to brain damage to what is just referred to as "retardation." Participating in these events not only trains the athletes to perform up to their highest potential, but it also infuses them with a sense of success, of competence, of achievement.

Recently, I heard a beautiful story about a race taking place in the Special Olympics. The athletes were lined up at the mark. The official yelled, "Ready, set, go!" and the athletes took off, all running as fast as their legs would carry them, with looks of determination, dedication and drive on their faces. All except one, that is. A young boy had tripped, immediately after starting, and had fallen into the dirt. He looked forlorn as he watched his peers race off without him.

Then, suddenly, a young girl who was running turned her head to see what had happened to the boy. As soon as she realized he fell, she turned around and ran back toward him. One by one, each of the athletes turned around to go back and look after the fallen boy. Soon all the runners were gathered around the young boy; they helped him to his feet as one girl brushed the dirt off his pants. Then, all the athletes held hands as they walked together, slowly, toward the finish line.

These are the people we refer to as "handicapped" or "retarded" or, euphemistically, "mentally and physically challenged." Yet, would we who have full use of all our limbs, whose brains function at their highest capacity, ever turn around in the middle of a race, giving up our long sought-after hope of winning and go back to look after someone who was down? Would we ever sacrifice getting to the top, being the best, winning it all, just to lend encouragement to another? Rarely.

We spend our lives pushing to be higher and higher, better and better. We want to be the best, to be the top, to be number one. But at what stake? What do we give up in the process? They say, *"The mark of a true man is not how tall he stands, but how frequently he bends down to help those in need."* How frequently are we willing to bend?

The goal of life is not the accumulation of more and more possessions, or more and more degrees. The point of life is to move toward God, to realize our oneness with Him. The point of life is to fill every moment with compassion, with love, with prayer and with service.

Yes, of course, we must go to work and we must do our best in every possible arena. Of course we must attempt to succeed; we must live up to our fullest potential. But, too frequently, we become narrow minded in what we see as our "potential." Is our potential merely financial, or academic or professional? Might we have another potential, a divine, compassionate, pious, devoted potential that is just waiting to blossom?

Let us vow to live up to every potential — not just those that confront us obviously in our daily life, but also those which may be hidden below the surface. The athletes may have thought, (and the audience may have thought as well) that their success, their achievement would be marked by how quickly they could run the 100 yards. However, the deep potential of these athletes was even greater than completing a "quick sprint." They chose compassion over competition; they chose unity over individual success; they chose to really show us what it means to be divine souls.

Let us take a lesson from these athletes, who are far less "handicapped" than most of the people in the world. Let us learn that each race in life may have two different paths for success; let us learn that compassion, love and unity are much more everlasting achievements than a blue ribbon.

Let us vow to turn our heads around frequently and see whether, perhaps, there is someone who needs our help.

REAL EDUCATION

Once there was a boat, sailing in the middle of the ocean. On the boat, were a philosopher, a scientist, a mathematician, and the boatman. The philosopher turned to the boatman and asked, "Do you know the nuances of Vedanta? Do you know the theories of Plato and Aristotle?" "No," replied the boatman. "I have never studied those things. I only know to take God's name in the morning when I wake up and at night before I sleep, and to try to keep Him with me all day long." The philosopher looked at him with disdain. "Well, then at least 30% of your life has been in vain."

Next, the scientist asked the boatman, "Do you know Einstein's Theory of Relativity? Do you know Newton's laws?" The boatman looked out at the reflection of the moon on the water. The light seemed to dance playfully off of the waves, touching first here, then there. He gently shook his head in response to the scientist's question. "No," he said. "I am not learned in that way. I have only learned to be kind, to give more than I receive, to be humble and pious." "Well," the scientist exclaimed. "Then at least 40% of your life has been in vain."

The mathematician then turned to the boatman. "You must at least know calculus? You must know how to compute advanced equations?" The boatman closed his eyes and entered a meditative trance. "No," he said softly, a smile creeping across his sun-weathered face. "I do not know those things." "Then, your life has been at least 50% in vain!" The mathematician retorted.

The four sat in silence for awhile, when suddenly the waves began to rise up furiously; the sky turned dark, obscuring the blanket of stars. The boat - thin and wooden - began to rock back and forth, up and down, with each thrust of the waves. The boatman fought diligently, using every muscle in his body, every skill he had to regain control over his boat. But the storm was winning the fight, and with each surge of the waves, the boatman became more and more convinced that the boat could not withstand this beating. As a wave lifted the boat high into the air, the boatman asked his passengers, "Do you know how to swim?" "NO!!!" they all cried at once. The wave dropped the boat, upside down, back in the raging water. The boatman watched sadly as the scientist, the philosopher and the mathematician drowned. "Well," he whispered "I think 100% of your lives have been in vain."

In this life, there are so many things to learn, so many things people say are important. Education is, of course, quite important. A doctor cannot operate if she doesn't know where the organs are, or how to sew a wound back up again. A scientist cannot perform experiments unless he knows which chemicals to use, and how much of each. An architect cannot design buildings without knowing what foundations and support are necessary.

However, in the big picture, these are not the lessons or

the education that truly liberate us. It is not this knowledge that saves us from drowning in the ocean. Only the knowledge of God can do that. Only love for Him, devotion to Him, and a life-vest inflated by Him can protect us in the raging sea of this world. For, many times in life, we feel like we are drowning. Many times we feel like we have swallowed so much water we can't breathe. It may seem as though our legs cannot possibly tread water for another minute.

At times like this we tend to turn to what we already know - more education, the acquisition of more possessions, the fulfillment of more sense pleasures. However, perhaps it is these that have caused our boat to capsize in the first place. Perhaps the ominous waves of the ocean are actually made up of our insatiable desires, of our purely academic educations, of our disregard for the Supreme Power behind and within everything.

Instead of making ourselves heavier and heavier, in which case we will surely drown, we must turn to the light, ever-present life vest around our bodies. It is knowledge of God, of how to truly live that will save us. The boatman knew how to see the stars; he knew how to watch God play in the light; he knew how to remain calm and serene even when challenged and insulted. He knew how to really swim.

DO YOUR DUTY

There was once a horrible drought. Year after year not a drop of rain fell on the arid ground. Crops died, and, as the land became parched, farmers gave up even planting their seeds. As the time of planting and tilling the ground came for the fourth rainless year in a row, the farmers of the region had given up hope and they sat listless, passing their time with playing cards and other distractions.

However, one lone farmer continued patiently to plant his seeds and sow and till his land. The other farmers poked fun at him and derided him as he continued daily to take care of his fruitless, barren land.

When they asked him the reason behind his senseless tenacity, he said, "I am a farmer and it is my dharma to plant and till my land. My dharma does not change simply due to whether the clouds rain or not. My dharma is my dharma and I must follow it regardless of how fruitful or fruitless it appears to be." The other farmers laughed at his wasteful effort, and went back to their homes to continue bemoaning the rainless sky and their fruitless land.

However, a passing rain cloud happened to be overhead when the faithful farmer was giving his answer to the others. The cloud heard the farmer's beautiful words and realized, "He's right. It is his dharma to plant the seeds and to till the land, and it is my dharma to release this water which I am holding in my cloud onto the ground." At that moment, inspired by the farmer's message, the cloud released all the water it was holding onto the farmer's land. This rain cloud then continued to spread the message of upholding one's dharma to the other rain clouds, and they too – upon realizing it was their dharma to rain – began to let go of the moisture in their midst. Soon, rain was pouring down upon the land, and the farmer's harvest was bountiful.

In life, we tend to expect results from our actions. If we do something well, we want to be rewarded. If we work, we want to be paid (whether financially or in some other way). We want to work only so long as the work reaps rewards. If the fruits cease to come, we decide the work is not "meant to be," and we abandon it.

However, that is not the message which Lord Krishna gives to Arjuna in the Gita. The message is that we must do our duty regardless of the fruits. We must live according to our dharma regardless of whether it is "successful." We must perform our duties for the simple fact that they are our duties.

Lord Krishna tells Arjuna to stand up and fight, and says that, even if he dies in the battle, he must still do his dharma. The Lord tells Arjuna that it is divine to die on the battlefield of life (meaning engaged in performing your duty). He explains that either way, Arjuna will "win." If the Pandavas win the battle, then they will obliterate the evil influence of the Kauravas and inherit the kingdom. If, on the other hand, the Kauravas win the battle and the Pandavas are killed, then they will go straight to the Lord's eternal abode, for they died in the service of Dharma.

Usually in life, we know what our duties are. We know our responsibilities. We can see the "right" thing to do. This is especially true if we take quiet time to meditate, reflect and contemplate. Yet, too frequently we walk away from doing the "right" thing or from performing our duty due to the uncertainty of the result. We don't want to "waste our time" or "look like a fool." We neglect our responsibilities by saying, "It doesn't matter any way." We shun our duties with words like, "Well, no one else is doing it, so why should I?"

This is not the way to live. We must realize that there is an enormous, infinite cosmic plan at work and we must all perform our allotted tasks to the best of our ability. Whether we actually succeed or fail in the venture should not be the biggest concern. True success comes not in a financial "win," but rather in the humble, tenacious, dedicated performance of our tasks.

Interestingly enough, when we act with righteousness and integrity, we find that others will follow. It is not that we are taken advantage of, as we frequently fear. Rather, if we set the divine example, others will follow suit. Just as the rain cloud followed the example of the tenacious farmer, so will those in our lives follow our own examples. If we act with honesty, we receive honesty. If we act with dedication and love, so we will receive dedication and love. If we fulfill our dharma, so will those around us learn to do the same.

Yet, even if we are the only ones acting piously, acting honestly, acting with devotion, it should not matter. Our lives, our happiness and our karma are individual entities. They are not dependent upon the response from others.

Therefore, we must all learn to stand up, have courage and keep performing our duties, regardless of whether it looks like success or failure will result. Through the fulfillment of our dharma we will achieve the greatest success in life – bliss, peace and enlightenment.

THE LEAKY BUCKET

In the very olden times, there was once a great king. This king had many, many servants to take care of every task. One particular servant was responsible for bringing water from the well to the King's table. However, it was a long journey from the castle to the well from which fresh, clean and pure water could be obtained. As this was the time before cars and other convenient machines, the servant carried two buckets - one attached to each end of a long stick - to transport water back to the castle. One of the buckets was new - it shone in the sunlight and it was perfect in every way. The other bucket was older and it had a small hole on one side that caused water to leak from it onto the ground, along the road back to the castle.

Thus, whenever the servant arrived back to the castle, although he had filled 2 buckets of water, he had only 1 and a half to present to the king. This caused the leaky bucket great distress. Twice a day when the servant picked up the buckets to go to the well, the older one would look longingly at the new one, "Oh, why can't I be as shiny and flawless as the other?" the bucket would bemoan. The leaky bucket would cast envious looks at the new bucket as not a single drop fell from its new, glistening metal.

It tried every possible way of shifting its weight, of rotating its sides to minimize the leakage, but all to no avail.

It could retain no more than half a bucket of water through the long walk back to the castle.

One day, the leaking bucket was distraught and cried out to the servant, "Why don't you just throw me away? I'm of no use to you. I can do barely half the work of your new bucket. You have to walk such a long way back and forth to the well and I leak out half of the water you fill me with. The king is such a good, noble, divine king. I want to serve him as well as your new bucket. But I can't; I can't even give him a full bucket of water."

The servant was very wise (sometimes wisdom lies hidden in places where we don't expect it). He said to the bucket, "Look down. Look below you on the path to the castle, the path upon which you leak your water." The bucket at first was too ashamed to look and see drops of precious water scattered on the ground. When it finally looked, however, it noticed a thick row of beautiful flowers - so many lush, blossoming varieties - lining the path with vibrancy and beauty.

"Every day I pick these flowers to decorate the king's table and his room," the servant said. "When I noticed that you were leaking, I planted seeds all along the path on your side of the road. Then, twice a day you come and water them. Now, they have grown and blossomed into the king's favorite centerpiece. He says their fragrance calms his mind and brings peace to his heart. So, see, you are not useless at all. Rather, you are serving two purposes - both to bring water (albeit half a bucket) and to bring beautiful flowers to the king's castle.

So many times in life we condemn ourselves for our failures, we compare ourselves unfavorably to others, we grieve over our own shortcomings, wishing that we could be different, more like someone else or some pre-conceived ideal. And as we do this, we blind ourselves to our real assets, to the flowers we are watering each day, to the real gifts we can give to the king.

God has given everyone a unique, special set of gifts and it is up to us to make the most of these. Some of us will be able to carry water without spilling a drop. Our gift to the world will be a full bucket of water. Others of us will be able to give only half a bucket of water, but we will line the world's paths with beautiful flowers and sweet fragrance. Let us never underestimate our potential or the significance of our own gifts. Let none of us ever feel just like a "leaky bucket."

# THE LITTLE THINGS IN LIFE

Once there was a saint who lived in the Himalayan forests. He lived in an ashram deep in a beautiful jungle where he spent his time in meditation and looking after the ashram.

Once a traveler came upon the saint and the ashram while trekking through the Himalayas. The young man started talking to the saint about the spiritual life. The young tourist asked him, "What did you do before you became enlightened?"

The saint replied, "I used to chop wood and carry water from the well."

The man then asked, "What do you do now that you have become enlightened?" The answer was simple. The saint replied, "I chop wood and carry water from the well."

The young man was puzzled. He said, "There seems to be no difference then. What was the point in going through all those years of sadhana in order to attain enlightenment if you still spend your days doing chores and menial tasks?"

The Master replied, "The difference is in me. The difference is not in my acts, it is in me—but because I have changed, all my acts have changed. Their significance has changed: the prose has become poetry, the stones have become sermons and matter has completely disappeared. Now there is only God and nothing else. Life now is liberation to me, it is nirvana."

So many people complain, "But my job is not spiritual." Or "How can I live a spiritual life while I have to care for children and a family?" The answer to a spiritual life is not in WHAT you're doing, but in HOW you're doing it. How attached are you to the details of what you're doing or how focused is your mind on God? Have stones become sermons? A spiritual life is not about renouncing work or renouncing chores or renouncing tasks that we may see as "beneath us." Rather, a spiritual life is about turning these tasks into tapasya, turning jobs into joy, turning stress into sadhana. This is a spiritual life.

People tend to think: first I'll complete my householder years and then I'll turn myself to God. Yes, in our culture, one dedicates one's life after retirement to God, to simplicity, to seva, to spirituality. But, you don't have to wait until you've retired in order to attain that glorious state. You can attain it while living IN the world. It's all a matter of the mind. Are you counting cars in front of you before you reach the tollbooth on the highway or are you counting the names of the Lord in your mind? Are you reciting lists of things to be done when you get home from the office, or are you reciting God's holy name? Is your tongue speaking angry remarks at your family, your co-workers and your neighbors or are you speaking only pure, calm, peaceful words?

Attaining enlightenment does not mean being out of the world or away from tasks. It means being IN the world, but not OF the world. It means DOING tasks, but not BEING the tasks.

Let us try – today – as we complete our daily routine to ask ourselves, "How would this routine be different if I were enlightened? How would my attitude change? How would my actions change?" Let us then pray to God for the strength to act accordingly. Then we'll know that we're really living a spiritual life, not merely relegating it to a few moments alone in the mandir at the end of the day.

TREASURE CHEST

There is a beautiful story of a beggar who lived all of his life under one tree. Each day he would go out into the villages and beg for just some dry bread crumbs to sustain his life. Then, he would come back to his tree and eat his bread or whatever scraps the villagers had given him that day. For forty years the beggar lived under the same tree, pleading with the people to give him some food. He'd walk to all the nearby villages, alternating days, begging for his nourishment. Slowly, day by day, he became weaker, and finally one day his body could no longer sustain itself and he passed quietly into death.

When the villagers found him, they decided to bury his ashes under the tree where he lived out his life. As they began to dig, in order to place his ashes deep in the ground, they found a treasure chest – full of gold, diamonds and jewels, a mere six inches below the ground.

For forty years, the beggar had lived, barely scraping by on his dry bread crumbs, sitting six inches above a treasure chest which would have rendered him as rich as a king. If only it had ever occurred to him to explore the depths of the Earth on which he sat, or to delve deeply into the recesses of his home – he would have discovered this treasure chest. But, he did not. Rather, he sat on the surface, suffering and withering away, day by day.

Too frequently in life we are also like this beggar – running here and there searching, begging for that which we need to fulfill our lives. Perhaps we are not begging for food or basic life necessities. More likely we are searching and yearning for peace, happiness or God. We go here, we beg there. We search this place, we search that place. But that priceless and yet crucial peace and happiness still elude us.

If only we would sit still for a moment and go deeper within, we would find that treasure chest. We don't even have to dig six inches. Just right within us, sitting in our heart, is God, and through our connection to Him, all of the riches of the world are bestowed upon us.

To the Indian youth, especially, you are all incredibly blessed. Your culture, your heritage and your traditions are a true treasure chest of meaning, understanding, wisdom and insight. Through opening this box of jewels you will definitely find the happiness, contentment and peace for which you are searching.

However, too frequently I see people running in the opposite direction in their fruitless search. They run from this workshop to that workshop, from this new trend to that new trend, all the while being frustrated in their search. Stop for a moment and look within. Go back to your roots, back to your heritage, back to the temple. Listen to the stories of your parents and grandparents. Perform aarti with deep devotion. Go to have the satsang and the darshan of visiting saints. Take a trip to India rather than to the beaches or ski slopes. Through this re-connection to your culture and your heritage you will find the key which will open the treasure chest.

But, never forget that the treasure chest is inside of you, flowing through your veins. It is not some external "thing" to be obtained or found. Rather, the divine joy is residing within you, in your heart, in your breath and in your blood.

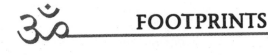

FOOTPRINTS

I heard a story once of a man who was a great devotee of God. Always throughout his life, God was his companion. He loved God more than anything else in all the world. When the man was very old, he lay in his bed one afternoon and had a dream. In this dream, he could see his entire life stretched out before him, as though it was the coastline along the ocean. And he could look back and see his footprints — deep impressions in the wet sand — marking the path he had walked in this life. As he looked back further and further, he could see that, in fact, there was not one, but 2 sets of footprints, side by side, along the edge of the ocean. He knew the other footprints were those of God, for he had felt God's presence beside him throughout his life.

But, then he saw something that woke him immediately from his dream; his heart beat fast and he could not hold back the tears. "God!" he cried out. "I just had a dream, and in this dream I could see the whole path of my life; I could see the footprints I left along the way. And beside my footprints, there were yours, for You walked with me, and..." Now the man was full of tears and could barely speak. "But, God, sometimes there was only one set of footprints, and when I looked, I could see that those were the times I was really fallen, really broken, when I needed You most. How, God, how could You leave me when I needed

You most? I thought You promised You'd be with me forever. Why did Your footprints disappear at the times I really needed You?"

Softly, gently, God laid a hand on the man's head, wiped away the tears. "My child, I promised to always be with you, and I have never left you for a second, not even while you slept. Those times when you see only one set of footprints, those darkest moments of your life, it was those times that I carried you in my arms."

There are times we feel abandoned by God, times we doubt His presence in our lives. It is easy to have faith when all is going well, easy to believe in a plan when that plan brings us joy and fulfillment. It is much more difficult to believe in the inherent goodness of the Planner when the plan causes agony. Do we all not, on some level, feel that when our lives are tough, that we have been left by God? But, oddly enough, it is those times that our faith will carry us through. It is truly those times in which we are being carried by God. Perhaps, as we get so much closer to him, as we move from walking beside Him to being in His arms, we actually feel His presence less, so we doubt it. Perhaps as the boundaries and borders between Him and us dissolve, and we simply become His children, perhaps that is when we truly lose ourselves in Him. As the otherness is gone, perhaps we feel less aware of the presence.

PIECES SENT
BY OTHERS

GIVE
BY: KAHLIL GIBRAN

You give but little when you give
of your possessions.
It is when you give of yourself that you truly give.
For what are your possessions but things you keep and
guard for fear you may need them tomorrow?

And tomorrow, what shall tomorrow bring to the over-
prudent dog burying bones in the trackless sand as he
follows the pilgrims to the holy city?
And what is fear of need but need itself?
Is not dread of thirst when your well is full,
the thirst that is unquenchable?

There are those who give little of the much they gave – and
they give it for recognition, and their hidden desire makes
their gifts unwholesome.
And there are those who have little and give it all.
These are the believers in life and the bounty of life, and
their coffer is never empty.

There are those who give with joy,
and that joy is their reward.
And there are those who give with pain,
and that pain is their baptism.
And there are those who give and have not pain in giving,
nor do they seek joy, nor give with mindfulness of virtue;
they give as in yonder valley the myrtle breathes its
fragrance into space.

Through the hand of such as these,
God speaks, and from behind their eyes
He smiles upon the earth.
It is well to give when asked,
But it is better to give unasked through understanding.

And to the open-handed the search for one who shall
receive is joy greater than giving.

And is there aught you would withhold?
All you have shall some day be given;
therefore give now, that the season of giving may be yours
and not your inheritors'.

You often say,
"I would give, but only to the deserving."
The trees in your orchard say not so,
nor the flocks in your pasture.
They give that they may live,
for to withhold is to perish.

Surely he who is worthy to receive his days and
his nights is worthy of all else from you.
And he who has deserved to drink from the ocean of life
deserves to fill his cup from your little stream.
And what desert greater shall there be,
than that which lies in the courage and the
confidence, nay the charity of receiving?

And who are you that men should rend their bosom and
unveil their pride, that you may see their worth naked
and their pride unabashed?

See first that you yourself deserve to be a giver,
and an instrument of giving
For, in truth it is life that gives into life – while you, who
deem yourself a giver, are but a witness.
And you receivers – and you are all receivers –
assume no weight of gratitude, lest you lay a yoke upon
yourself and upon he who gives;
rather rise together with the giver on his gifts as on wings.

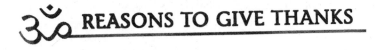# REASONS TO GIVE THANKS

If you woke up this morning with more health than illness, you are more blessed than the million who will not survive the week.

If you have never experienced the danger of battle, the loneliness of imprisonment, the agony of torture or the pangs of starvation, you are ahead of 500 million people around the world.

If you attend a temple or church meeting without fear of harassment, arrest or torture of death, you are more blessed that almost three billion people in the world.

If you have food in your refrigerator, clothes on your back, a roof over your head and a place to sleep, you are richer than 75% of this world.

If you have money in the bank, in your wallet, and spare change in a dish someplace, you are among the top 8% of the world's wealthy.

If your parents are still married and alive, you are very rare, even in the United States.

If you hold up your head with a smile on your face and are truly thankful, you are blessed because the majority can, but most do not.

If you can hold someone's hand, hug them or even touch them on the shoulder, you are blessed because you can offer God's healing touch.

If you prayed yesterday and today, you are in the minority because you believe in God's willingness to hear and answer prayer.

If you can read this message, you are more blessed than over two billion people in the world that cannot read anything at all.

WHAT A DIFFERENCE A DAY MAKES
IN THE WAKE OF SEPTEMBER 11, 2001

On Monday we emailed jokes
On Tuesday we did not

On Monday we thought that we were secure
On Tuesday we learned better

On Monday we were talking about heroes as being athletes
On Tuesday we relearned who our heroes are

On Monday we were irritated that our rebate checks had not
arrived
On Tuesday we gave money away to people we had never met

On Monday there were people fighting against praying in schools
On Tuesday you would have been hard pressed to find a school
where someone was not praying

On Monday people argued with their kids about picking up their
room
On Tuesday the same people could not get home fast enough to
hug their kids

On Monday people were upset that they had to wait 6 minutes in a fast food drive through line
On Tuesday people didn't care about waiting up to 6 hours to give blood for the dying

On Monday we waved our flags signifying our cultural diversity
On Tuesday we waved only the American flag

On Monday there were people trying to separate each other by race, sex, color and creed
On Tuesday they were all holding hands

On Monday we men or women, black or white, old or young, rich or poor, gay or straight, Christian or non-Christian.
On Tuesday we were Americans

On Monday politicians argued about budget surpluses
On Tuesday grief stricken they sang 'God Bless America'

On Monday the President was going to Florida to read to children
On Tuesday he returned to Washington to protect our children

On Monday we had families
On Tuesday we had orphans

On Monday people went to work as usual
On Tuesday they died

ॐ 12 WAYS TO OVERCOME STRESS BY:
H.H. DADA J.P. VASWANI

1. Fill your minds with thoughts of God: wake up in the morning with a great thought of a Great One or a text from a scripture dear to you.

2. Close the day by reading some positive literature.

3. Practice the presence of God.

4. Never neglect your daily appointment with God.

5. Breathe out peace, love and blessing to all.

6. Forgive before forgiveness is asked.

7. Help others.

8. Be relaxed at all times.

9. Develop a healthy sense of humour.

10. Always see the bright side of things.

11. Develop faith in the goodness and caring power of God.

12. In all conditions of life let the words-- Thank you, God-- be on your lips all the time.

GET A LIFE

This is a commencement speech made by Anna Quindlen at Villanova:

It's a great honor for me to be the third member of my family to receive an honorary doctorate from this great university. It's an honor to follow my great Uncle Jim, who was a gifted physician, and my Uncle

Jack, who is a remarkable businessman. Both of them could have told you something important about their professions, about medicine or commerce. I have no specialized field of interest or expertise, which puts me at a disadvantage talking to you today. I'm a novelist. My work is human nature. Real life is all I know.

Don't ever confuse the two, your life and your work. The second is only part of the first. Don't ever forget what a friend once wrote Senator Paul Tsongas when the senator decided not to run for re-election because he had been diagnosed with cancer: "No man ever said on his deathbed I wish I had spent more time at the office." Don't ever forget the words my father sent me on a postcard last year: "If you win the rat race, you're still a rat." Or what John Lennon wrote before he was gunned down in the driveway of the Dakota: "Life is what happens while you are busy making other plans."

You will walk out of here this afternoon with only one thing that no one else has. There will be hundreds of people out there with your same degree; there will be thousands of people doing what you want to do for a living. But you will be the only person alive who has sole custody of your life. Your particular life. Your entire life. Not just your life at a desk, or your life on a bus, or in a car, or at the computer. Not just the life of your mind, but the life of your heart. Not just your bank account, but your soul.

People don't talk about the soul very much anymore. It's so much easier to write a resume than to craft a spirit. But a resume is a cold comfort on a winter night, or when you're sad, or broke, or lonely, or when you've gotten back the test results and they're not so good.

Here is my resume: I am a good mother to three children. I have tried never to let my profession stand in the way of being a good parent. I no longer consider myself the center of the universe.

I show up. I listen. I try to laugh. I am a good friend to my husband. I have tried to make marriage vows mean what they say. I am a good friend to my friends, and they to me. Without them, there would be nothing to say to you today, because I would be a cardboard cutout. But I call them on the phone, and I meet them for lunch. I would be rotten, or at best mediocre at my job, if those other things were not true. You cannot be really first rate at your work if your work is all you are. So here's what I wanted to tell you today:

Get a life. A real life, not a manic pursuit of the next promotion, the bigger paycheck, the larger house. Do you think you'd care so very much about those things if you blew an aneurysm one afternoon, or found a lump in your breast?

Get a life in which you notice the smell of salt water pushing itself on a breeze over Seaside Heights, a life in which you stop and watch how a red tailed hawk circles over the water or the way a baby scowls with concentration when she tries to pick up a Cheerio with her thumb and first finger. Get a life in which you are not alone.

Find people you love, and who love you. And remember that love is not leisure, it is work. Pick up the phone. Send an e-mail. Write a letter.

Get a life in which you are generous. And realize that life is the best thing ever, and that you have no business taking it for granted. Care so deeply about its goodness that you want to spread it around. Take money you would have spent on beers and give it to charity. Work in a soup kitchen. Be a big brother or sister. All of you want to do well. But if you do not do good too, then doing well will never be enough.

It is so easy to waste our lives, our days, our hours, our minutes. It is so easy to take for granted the color of our kids' eyes, the way the melody in a symphony rises and falls and disappears and rises again. It
is so easy to exist instead of to live.

I learned to live many years ago. Something really, really bad happened to me, something that changed my life in ways that, if I had my druthers, it would never have been changed at all. And what I learned from it is what, today, seems to be the hardest lesson of all.

I learned to love the journey, not the destination. I learned that it is not a dress rehearsal, and that today is the only guarantee you get. I learned to look at all the good in the world and try to give some of it back because I believed in it, completely and utterly. And I tried to do that, in part, by telling others what I had learned. By telling them this:

Consider the lilies of the field. Look at the fuzz on a baby's ear. Read in the backyard with the sun on your face. Learn to be happy . And think of life as a terminal illness, because if you do, you will live it with joy and passion as it ought to be lived.

 AUDREY HEPBURN'S BEAUTY SECRETS

For attractive lips, speak words of kindness.

For lovely eyes, seek out the good in people.

For a lovely figure, share your food with the hungry.

For beautiful hair, let a child run his or her fingers through it once a day.

For poise, walk with the knowledge that you'll never walk alone.

People, even more than things, have to be restored, renewed, revived, reclaimed and redeemed.

Never throw out anybody.

Remember, if you ever need a helping hand, you'll find one at the end of your arm.

As you grow older, you will discover that you have two hands, one for helping yourself, and one for helping others.

The beauty of a woman is not in the clothes she wears, the figure that she carries, or the way she combs her hair.

The beauty of a woman must be seen from in her eyes, Because that is the doorway to her heart.

The beauty of a woman is not in a facial mole, But true beauty in a woman is reflected in her soul.

It is the caring that she lovingly gives, the passion that she shows, and the beauty of a woman with passing years only grows!

LETTER FROM GABRIEL GARCIA MARQUEZ WHEN HE RETIRED FROM PUBLIC LIFE DUE TO CANCER

If for an instant God were to forget that I am rag doll and gifted me with a piece of life, possibly I wouldn't say all that I think, but rather I would think of all that I say. I would value things, not for their worth but for what they mean. I would sleep little, dream more, understanding that for each minute we close our eyes we lose sixty seconds of light.

I would walk when others hold back, I would wake when others sleep. I would listen when others talk, and how I would enjoy a good chocolate ice cream! If God were to give me a piece of life, I would dress simply, throw myself face first into the sun, baring not only my body but also my soul.

My God, if I had a heart, I would write my hate on ice, and wait for the sun to show. Over the stars I would paint with a Van Gogh dream, a Benedetti poem, and a Serrat song would be the serenade I'd offer to the moon. With my tears I would water roses, to feel the pain of their thorns, and the red kiss of their petals...

My God, if I had a piece of life... I wouldn't let a single day pass without telling the people I love that I love them. I would convince each woman and each man that they are my favorites, and I would live in love with love. I would show men how very wrong they are to think that they cease to be in love when they grow old, not knowing that they grow old when they cease to be in love! To a child I shall give wings, but I shall let him learn to fly on his own. I would teach the old that death does not come with old age, but with forgetting.

I have learned that everyone wants to live on the peak of the mountain, without knowing that real happiness is in how it is scaled. I have learned that when a newborn child squeezes for the first time with his tiny fist his father's finger, he has him trapped forever. I have learned that a man has the right to look down on another only when he has to help the other get to his feet.

I have learned so many things, but in truth they won't be of much use, for when I keep them within this suitcase, unhappily shall I be dying.

GABRIEL GARCIA MARQUEZ

 # PARADOX OF OUR TIMES

The paradox of our time in history is that:

we have taller buildings but shorter tempers;
wider freeways, but narrower viewpoints.
We spend more, but have less;
we buy more but enjoy less

We have bigger houses and smaller families,
more conveniences, but less time;
we have more degrees, but less sense;
more knowledge, but less judgment;
more experts, yet more problems,
more medicine, but less wellness.

We drink too much, smoke too much,
spend too recklessly,
laugh too little,
drive too fast,
get too angry,
stay up too late, get up too tired,
read too little, watch TV too much, and pray too seldom.

We have multiplied our possessions,
but reduced our values.
We talk too much, love too seldom,
and hate too often.

We've learned how to make a living, but not a life,
we've added years to life not life to years.
We've been all the way to the moon and back, but have
trouble crossing the street to meet a new neighbor.
We conquered outer space but not inner space.
We've done larger things, but not better things.

We've cleaned up the air, but polluted the soul.
We've conquered the atom, but not our prejudice.
We write more, but learn less.
We plan more, but accomplish less.
We've learned to rush, but not to wait.

We build more computers to hold more information to
produce more copies than ever, but we communicateless
and less.

These are the times of fast foods and slow digestion; big
men and small character; steep profits and shallow
relationships.

These are the days of two incomes but more divorce,
fancier houses but broken homes.

These are days of quick trips, disposable diapers,
throwaway morality, one-night stands, overweight bodies,
and pills that do everything from cheer to quiet, to kill.

It is a time when there is much in the show window and
nothing in the stockroom.

 **I'VE LEARNED**

I've learned that no matter what happens, or how bad it seems today, life does go on, and it will be better tomorrow.

I've learned that you can tell a lot about a person by the way he/she handles these three things: a rainy day, lost luggage, and tangled Christmas tree lights.

I've learned that regardless of your relationship with your parents, you'll miss them when they're gone from your life.

I've learned that making a "living" is not the same as making a "life."

I've learned that life sometimes gives you a second chance.

I've learned that you shouldn't go through life with a catcher's mit on both hands. You need to be able to throw something back.

I've learned that if you pursue happiness, it will elude you. But if you focus on your family, your friends, the needs of others, your work and doing the best you can, happiness will find you.

I've learned that whenever I decide something with an open heart, I usually make the right decision.
I've learned that even when I have pains, I don't have to be one.

I've learned that every day you should reach out and touch someone. People love that human touch - holding hands, a warm hug, or just a friendly pat on the back.

People will forget what you said, people will forget what you did, but people will never forget how you made them feel.........

ॐ WITHOUT THE MASTER
BY KABIR

A temple roof
Cannot stay up without rafters;
So without Nam
How can one cross the ocean?
Without a vessel
Water cannot be kept;
So without a Saint
Man cannot be saved from doom.
Woe to him
Who thinks not of God,
Whose mind and heart
Remain absorbed in ploughing
The field of the senses.

Without a ploughman
Land cannot be tilled,
Without a thread
Jewels cannot be strung,
Without a knot
The sacred tie cannot be made;
So without a Saint
Man cannot be saved from doom.

A child cannot be born
Without father and mother,
Clothes cannot be washed
Without water,
There can be no horseman
Without a horse;
So without a Master
None can reach the court of the Lord.

Without music
There can be no wedding;
Rejected by her husband,
A bad woman suffers misery;
So man suffers
Without a Saint.
Says Kabir, My friend,
Only one thing attain:
Become a gurumukh
That you not die again.

A.G., Gond, p.8 72

# WATCH AND LISTEN CAREFULLY

The man whispered, "God, speak to me" and
a meadowlark sang.
But the man did not hear.

So the man yelled "God, speak to me!"
And the thunder rolled across the sky.
But the man did not listen.

The man looked around and said, "God, let me see you."
And a star shined brightly.
But the man did not notice.

Then the man shouted, "God, show me a miracle!"
And a life was born.
But the man did not know.

So the man cried out in despair,
"Touch me God, and let me know you are here!"
Whereupon, God reached down and touched the man.
But the man brushed the butterfly away and walked on.

I AM THANKFUL:

For the teenager who is not doing dishes,
but is watching TV,
Because it means he is at home and not on the streets.

For the taxes that I pay,
Because it means that I am employed.

For the mess to clean up after a party,
Because it means I have been surrounded by friends.

For the clothes that fit a little too snugly,
Because it means I have enough to eat.

For my shadow that watches me work,
Because it means that I am out in the sunshine.

For a lawn that needs mowing, windows that need
cleaning, and gutters that need fixing,
Because it means that I have a home.

For all the complaining I hear about the Government,
Because it means that we have freedom of speech.

For the parking spot I find at the far end of the parking lot,
Because it means I am capable of walking and that I have
been blessed with transportation.

For my huge heating bill,
Because it means that I am warm.

For the lady behind me in church who sings off key,
Because it means that I can hear.

For the pile of laundry and ironing I have to do,
Because it means I have clothes to wear.

For the weariness and
aching muscles at the end of the day,
Because it means that I am capable of working hard and
that I have employment.

For the alarm that goes off early in the morning,
Because it means that I am alive.

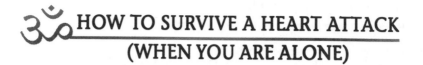

HOW TO SURVIVE A HEART ATTACK
(WHEN YOU ARE ALONE)

Let's say you're driving home after an unusually hard day on the job. Suddenly you start experiencing severe pain in your chest that starts to radiate out into your arm and up into your jaw.

What can you do? Without help the person whose heart stops beating properly and who begins to feel faint, has only about 10 seconds left before losing consciousness.

However, these victims can help themselves by coughing repeatedly and very vigorously.

A deep breath should be taken before each cough, and the cough must be deep and prolonged, as when producing sputum from deep inside the chest.

A breath and a cough must be repeated about every two seconds without let up until help arrives, or until the heart is felt to be beating normally again.

Deep breaths get oxygen into the lungs and coughing movements squeeze the heart and keep the blood circulating. The squeezing pressure on the heart also helps it regain normal rhythm. In this way, heart attack victims can get to a phone and, between breaths, call for help.

From: Health Cares   Rochester General Hospital

BILL GATES' 11 RULES
FOR STUDENTS

Rule 1 - Life is not fair; get used to it!

Rule 2 - The world won't care about your self-esteem. The world will expect you to accomplish something BEFORE you feel good about yourself.

Rule 3 - You will NOT make 40 thousand dollars a year right out of high school. You won't be a vice president with a car phone, until you earn both.

Rule 4 - If you think your teacher is tough, wait till you get a boss. He doesn't have tenure.

Rule 5 - Flipping burgers is not beneath your dignity. Your grandparents had a different word for burger flipping; they called it opportunity.

Rule 6 - Your school may have done away with winners and losers, but life has not. In some schools, they have abolished failing grades; they'll give you as many times as you want to get the right answer. This doesn't bear the slightest resemblance to ANYTHING in real life.

Rule 7 - Before you were born, your parents weren't as boring as they are now. They got that way from paying your bills, cleaning your clothes and listening to you talk about how cool you are. So, before you save the rainforest from the parasites of your parents generation, try "delousing" the closet in your own room.

Rule 8 - If you mess up, it's not your parents' fault, so don't whine about your mistakes, learn from them.

Rule 9 - Life is not divided into semesters. You don't get summers off, and very few employers are interested in helping you find yourself. Do that on your own time.

Rule 10 - Television is NOT a real life. In real life, people actually have to leave the coffee shop and go to jobs.

Rule 11 - Be nice to nerds. Chances are you'll end up working for one.

PERFECTION

In Brooklyn, New York, Chush is a school that caters to learning disabled children. Some children remain in Chush for their entire school career, while others can be mainstreamed into conventional schools. At a

Chush fund-raising dinner, the father of a Chush child delivered a speech that would never be forgotten by all who attended. After extolling the school and its dedicated staff, he cried out, "Where is the perfection in my son, Shaya? Everything God does is done with perfection. But my child cannot understand things as other children do. My child cannot remember facts and figures as other children do. Where is God's perfection?" The audience was shocked by the question, pained by the father's anguish and stilled by the piercing query.

"I believe," the father answered, "that when God brings a child like this into the world, the perfection that he seeks is in the way people react to this child." He then told the following story about his son, Shaya:"One afternoon, Shaya and I walked past a park where some boys Shaya knew were playing baseball.

Shaya asked, 'Do you think they will let me play?" I knew that my son was not at all athletic, and that most boys would not want him on their team. But I understood that if my his son was chosen to play, it would give him a comfortable sense of belonging. I approached one of the boys in the field and asked if Shaya could play. The boy looked around for guidance from his teammates. Getting none, he took matters into his own hands, and said, 'We are losing by six runs and the game is in the eighth inning. I guess he can be on our team, and we'll try to put him up to bat in the ninth inning.' I was ecstatic as Shaya smiled broadly.

Shaya was to go put on a glove,and go out to play short-center-field. In the bottom of the eight inning,Shaya's team scored a few runs, but was still behind by three. In the bottom of the ninth inning, Shaya's team scored again, and, now with two outs and the bases loaded with the potential winning run on base, Shaya was scheduled to be up. Would the team actually let Shaya bat at this juncture and give away its chance to win the game? Surprisingly, Shaya was given the bat. Everyone knew that it was all but impossible because Shaya didn't even know how to hold the bat, properly,let alone hit with it.

However, as Shaya stepped up to the plate the pitcher moved a few steps to lob the ball in softly so Shaya should at least be able to make contact. The first pitch came, and Shay swung, clumsily, and missed. One of Shaya's teammates came up to Shaya and, together they held the bat and faced the pitcher, waiting for the next pitch. The pitcher again took a few steps forward to toss the ball softly toward Shaya.

As the pitch came in, Shaya and his teammate swung at the ball,and,together they hit a slow ground ball to the pitcher. The pitcher picked up the soft grounder, and could easily have thrown the ball to the first baseman. Shaya would have been out, and that would have ended the game.

Instead, the pitcher took the ball and threw it on a high arc to right field, far beyond the reach of the first baseman. Everyone started yelling, 'Shaya, run to first. Run to first' Never in his life had Shaya run to first. He scampered down the baseline, wide- eyed and startled. By the time he reached first base, the right fielder had theball. He could have thrown the ball to the second baseman who would tag out Shaya, who was still running. But the right fielder understood what the pitcher's intentions were, so he threw the ball high, and far over the 3rd baseman's head. Everyone yelled,'Run to second, run to second.' Shaya ran towards second base as the runners ahead of him deliriously circled the bases towards home. As Shaya reached second base, the opposing short-stop ran to him, turned him in the direction of third base and shouted, 'Run to third.' As Shaya rounded third, the boys from both teams ran behind him, screaming, 'Shaya run home.'

Shaya ran home, stepped on home plate, and all 18 boys lifted him on their shoulders and made him the hero, as he had just hit a "grandslam" and won the game for his team.

"That day," said the father, softly, "those 18 boys reached their level of God's perfection."

INDIA HERITAGE RESEARCH FOUNDATION (IHRF)

Pujya Swami Chidanand Saraswatiji (Muniji) is the founder and chairman of India Heritage Research Foundation, a non-profit charitable organization dedicated to humanitarian and cultural projects. Founded in 1987, IHRF is committed to preserving the timeless wisdom and ageless grandeur of Indian culture. By weaving together ancient tradition, cultural history, a wide range of non-discriminatory charitable services, and inspiring youth programs, IHRF has created a tapestry of true, universal beauty.

The Encyclopedia of Hinduism

IHRF is currently completing the revolutionary project of compiling the first Encyclopedia of Hinduism in history. The Encyclopedia will mark the first time that the urgent need is met for an authentic, objective and insightful well of information, capturing both the staples and the spices of Indian tradition and culture. This 18 volume work is currently in the final stages of research and compilation by over 1250 internationally renowned scholars. We expect to have the manuscript completed by the end of 2002.

The Encyclopedia of Hinduism will be a significant landmark, encompassing the entire spectrum of   called Bharat.

While its current focus is on the momentous Encyclopedia Project, the picture of IHRF is significantly vaster. The foundation is dedicated to youth, education, spirituality, culture, inter-faith harmony, health care and ecology. To this end, it runs hospitals, schools, training centers, large-scale spiritual and cultural events, tree-plantation and clean-up programs, conferences geared toward inter-faith harmony, summer camps, and international youth awareness programs. Additionally, it sponsors (both financially and otherwise) dozens of educational and medical institutions that are already established but suffering from lack of resources.

Following are examples of only a few of the numerous ways that IHRF's arms embrace humanity:

Y.E.S. — Youth Education Services

Many villages throughout India are oceans of poverty and illiteracy. The influx of technology, commerce, education and metropolitanism that has flooded most of India's cities since Independence, seems to have not even touched these villages. They exist as they did centuries ago. However, one crucial change has occurred. Now, basic education and marketable skills are absolute necessities in order to subsist in even the smallest communities. Hence, those who lack this education and training, go to sleep hungry each night.

In the midst of this ocean of destitution, there are islands of light, islands of knowledge, islands of hope. The YES schools are some of these islands. The YES program encompasses dozens of  children's schools, numerous women's vocational training programs, an orphanage/gurukul and a Veda Shala.

However, in addition to a greater potential for their future, the children and women in the YES programs are being given a better today. They receive medical care. Ecological hygiene projects are set up in their villages. The children are given school supplies and uniforms. The women receive all necessary tools and equipment to tailor clothing, produce local handicrafts, learn typing etc. The orphaned children receive not only shelter but also the love, nurturing and essential values which are so crucial to a healthy up-bringing.

The children and women in the YES program are given not only an education, but they are also given the priceless gifts of hope and faith.

The YES program is dedicated to providing poor, illiterate and orphaned children a positive, nurturing environment, and to giving them the best chance possible to live a life free from destitution and despair.

Orphanage/Gurukul

One visit to India is sufficient to see the urgent, dire need for orphanages. However, simple shelters with food, beds and babysitters are not sufficient. These children need not only

to be fed and sheltered. Rather, they also need to be educated and trained so they can become productive members of society. They need to be inculcated with values, ethics and spirituality which will make them torchbearers of Indian culture.

The Parmarth Gurukul/Orphanage (sponsored by IHRF) serves as a place where these orphans and impoverished children are housed as well as educated, cultured and filled with crucial values such as non-violence, truth and seva.

Their days are filled with yoga, meditation, Vedic chanting, reading of scriptures, mathematics, seva and special programs designed to instill in them essential sanskaras.

Looks of hopelessness have become looks of optimism and hope. Lightless eyes have become bright, shining eyes. Feelings of destitution and despair have become feelings of pride, faith and enthusiasm.

There are currently 100 young boys living in the Parmarth Gurukul/orphanage, where their days are spent obtaining a full-fledged academic education as well as a complete Vedic education including chanting, scriptural memorization, pujas, and other rituals, sandhya, yoga and meditation. We have plans to bring in another 200 boys by the end of 2002.

Mansarover Ashram and Clinic

Under the guidance, inspiration and vision of Pujya Swami Chidanand Saraswatiji (Muniji), IHRF has taken on the

new project of building an ashram, hospital and oxygen plant in the holy land of Lake Mansarovar and Mt. Kailash in Tibet.

There are currently no medical facilities for hundreds of kilometers.

People frequently suffer from basic, treatable ailments due to lack of medical attention. There is not even an indoor place to stay. Therefore, after undertaking a yatra to the sacred land in 1998, Pujya Swami Chidanand Saraswatiji (Muniji) took a vow that — by the grace of God — He would do something for the local people (who don't even have running water) and for all the pilgrims who travel there.

Now, the tourist rest house and clinic have been built and will be officially inaugurated in June 2002 bythe hand of H.H. Sri Shankaracharyaji Kanchi Kaam Koti, H.H. Sri Shankaracharyaji Bhanpura Peeth, H.H. Swami Gurusharananandji Maharaj, H.H. Sant Shri Rameshbhai Oza and other revered saints and dignitaries.

Further, the contract states that for all future projects in the region (including schools, vocational training program, health care

programs, sanitation programs), the government of Tibet/ China will give first priority to IHRF to sponsor the project. Thus, this will be the spring board for other much-needed humanitarian projects in the area.

The project is truly the grace of God and will be a divine gift to the holy land, to all the impoverished Tibetans who live there, and to all the pious pilgrims who cross oceans and continents in order to have a glimpse of the abode of Lord Shiva.

Disaster Relief

IHRF is actively engaged in assisting those whose lives have been shattered by natural catastrophes.

In March 1999, a disastrous 6.8 magnitude earthquake struck in the sacred Himalayas, killing hundreds and leaving thousands homeless.

Since the pre-dawn hours after the tragedy, Pujya Swamiji has used all possible resources to provide disaster relief. Over the course of three separate trips, IHRF has (with the cooperation of Parmarth Niketan and with the assistance of generous donors) provided over 500 families with blankets, tarpaulins, lanterns, clothing, medicine and food supplies.

Additionally, we have also built eleven schools in this disaster-struck region, and we are making concrete plans to re-build numerous homes which were destroyed.

On October 29, 1999, a catastrophic cyclone tore through the coast of Orissa, killing tens of thousands and leaving even more homeless.

We immediately sponsored the re-building of 8 schools and a medical facility which had been destroyed in the cyclone. Within a few short months, these schools and medical clinic were renovated, rebuilt and repaired to a better state than they were before the cyclone.

Ekal Vidyalaya: Tribal Education

IHRF -- in cooperation with Friends of Tribals Society and other charitable institutions -- is building schools in rural, tribal India.

These children live in lands that time forgot. Their villages are islands of indigence and stagnation amidst an ocean of economic and technologic growth. They have probably never seen an electric light-bulb, nor heard the sound of a telephone, nor traveled in a car or train. They, of course, can also neither read nor write nor compute simple arithmetic.

The population of India is burgeoning out of control — the rural, tribal peoples are already being dominated, oppressed and defrauded by those hungry for land, crops and cheap labor. Left to their own simple, uneducated ways, they will never be able to survive. Through the Parmarth Shiksha Mandir (Ekal Vidyalala) project, we are bringing the light of education as well as invaluable sanskars to our 70 million tribal brothers and sisters suffering in darkness.

Our goal is to bring education to the illiterate, understanding to the bewildered, strength to the weak, means to the poverty-stricken and hope to the downtrodden. Through this noble project we can bring the light of knowledge, inspiration and hope to the children who will stand as the torchbearers of our nation.

Ecological "Clean, Green and Serene" Programs

IHRF runs programs dedicated to cultivating an awareness of environmental sanctity as well as with the mission of restoring Mother Earth's natural balance. Its focus is currently on preserving holy pilgrimage areas, called Tirthas.

Currently, IHRF is running two "Clean, Green and Serene Programs," one in Rishikesh, Himalayas and one in Varanasi. In these urgent and noble programs, IHRF pledges to clean up the holy banks of our Mother Ganga. Although we worship Her as mother, we throw our trash in her waters and on her ghats. We pollute the pathways running beside her current.

In order to immediately remedy this situation and restore Mother Ganga to her rightful state of sublime beauty, we have instituted "Clean, Green and Serene" programs in these two holy cities.

The Rishikesh program has been running in cooperation with Parmarth Niketan Ashram (the largest institution in Rishikesh), and with the generosity of dedicated donors.

The Varanasi "Clean, Green and Serene" program was officially inaugurated over the New Millennium Eve of December 31, 1999. In this noble program, we – in are supporting and assisting Parmarth Ganga Seva Nidhi to institute daily aarti and clean up of Mother Ganga programs

---

Through these programs, our ancient, holy pilgrimage cities will be restored to their rightful state of purity, sanctity and spiritual sublimity.

In general, IHRF is the backbone of numerous charitable organizations and provides a vast range of services. The Foundation is dedicated to bringing food to the hungry, medicine to the sick, and peace to the troubled. IHRF does not discriminate on the basis of race, religion, caste, creed, gender or nationality.

Additionally, all of its services are open to all and free to all. From emergency relief for disaster victims to the building of orphanages to improving care for the handicapped, IHRF embraces the whole of humanity and seeks to heal whatever ails God's children

PARMARTH NIKETAN ASHRAM RISHIKESH, INDIA

H.H. Swami Chidanand Saraswatiji (Pujya Muniji) is president of Parmarth Niketan Ashram in Rishikesh, India, a true, spiritual haven, lying on the holy banks of Mother Ganga, in the lap of the lush Himalayas.

Parmarth Niketan is the largest ashram in Rishikesh. Parmarth Niketan provides its thousands of pilgrims – who come from all corners of the Earth – with a clean, pure and sacred atmosphere as well as abundant, beautiful gardens. With over 1000 rooms, the facilities are a perfect blend of modern amenities and traditional, spiritual simplicity.

The daily activities at Parmarth Niketan include morning universal prayers, daily yoga and meditation classes, daily satsang and lecture programs, kirtan, world renowned Ganga aarti at sunset, as well as full Nature Cure and

Ayurvedic treatment and training.

Additionally, there are frequently special cultural and spiritual programs given by visiting revered saints, acclaimed musicians, spiritual and social leaders and others.

Additionally, there are frequent camps in which pilgrims come from across the world to partake in intensive courses on yoga, meditation, pranayama, stress management, acupressure, Reiki and other Indian, ancient sciences.

Parmarth Niketan is managed by the Swami Shukdevanand Trust, a registered non-profit organization, founded in 1942 and dedicated to charity, conservation, and youth/education programs. Parmarth Niketan is the headquarters of this trust; hence it is from here, flowing from the divine light of Pujya Swamiji, that the majority of the services come.

Further, Parmarth Niketan's charitable activities and services make no distinctions on the basis of caste, color, gender, creed or nationality. Instead they emphasize unity, harmony, peace, global integrity, health, and the holistic connection between the body, mind and spirit.

True to its name, Parmarth Niketan is dedicated to the welfare of all. Everything is open to all and free to all.